Dark Shadows of Vietnam is a collection of personal observations and stories forged in the horrific fighting of the Vietnam War. Told with compelling simplicity, the harsh reality of the experiences remind the readers of the aching youthfulness of the men who sacrificed their innocence and their lives for a cause that brought opprobrium on them when they returned home, haunted their subsequent lives, and which continues to be a perplexing and agonizing episode in US history.

—LOURDES THUESEN
Editor

I am a two-tour veteran of Vietnam. I believe this man is so real. He had to get this off his chest.

—DENNIS LEE THOMAS
4th Infantry, US Army

THE DARK SHADOWS
OF
VIETNAM

TRUE STORIES AND PERSONAL VIEWS

THE DARK SHADOWS

OF

VIETNAM

1966–1967

JOSEPH W. BABINE

UNITED STATES MARINE CORPS

TATE PUBLISHING
AND **ENTERPRISES**, LLC

Published by Tate Publishing & Enterprises, LLC
127 E. Trade Center Terrace | Mustang, Oklahoma 73064 USA
1.888.361.9473 | www.tatepublishing.com

Tate Publishing is committed to excellence in the publishing industry. The company reflects the philosophy established by the founders, based on Psalm 68:11,
"The Lord gave the word and great was the company of those who published it."

Book design copyright © 2012 by Tate Publishing, LLC. All rights reserved.
Cover design by Joel Uber
Interior design by April Marciszewski
Map illustrations by Max Seabaugh of Max Design Studio, Lake County, California

Published in the United States of America

ISBN: 978-1-62024-177-6
1. Biography & Autobiography / Military
2. Biography & Autobiography / Historical
12.05.07

DEDICATION

To all the Marines I served with in the United States
Marine Corps and Vietnam

ACKNOWLEDGEMENTS

Sharleen Schekat, for helping me through the years with her computer work.

Lourdes Thuesen, for her editing and expertise in shaping my book.

Dennis Lee Thomas, a Vietnam veteran, for pushing me to write both the stories I tell him, as well as my personal views and opinions.

Bonnie, my wife, for putting up with me through the years of writing my book.

TABLE OF CONTENTS

MAPS _____ 13

INTRODUCTION _____ 17

CHAPTER 1 _____ 19

    Growing Up_____ 19

    The Family Plot_____ 22

    United States Marine Corps _____ 24

    Gulf of Tonkin _____ 28

CHAPTER 2 _____ 30

    Areas Served_____ 30

    Trouble before Trouble_____ 33

    The Landing _____ 35

CHAPTER 3 _____ 38

    What Goes Around Comes Around_____ 38

    The Cards _____ 40

    The Trail _____ 44

    The Hill _____ 47

CHAPTER 4 _____ 54

    Nine Hundred Killed _____ 54

    Miracle Hit _____ 55

    One-man Patrols _____ 56

CHAPTER 5 _____ 61

    Lang Vei _____ 61

    Inspection of Perimeter _____ 63

    Hot and Cold_____ 64

CHAPTER 6 _____ 68

    Fragging _____ 68

    The Ears _____ 72

    Chieu Hoi _____ 75

CHAPTER 7 _____ 79

    A Different Kind of Marine_____ 79

    False Ambush_____ 82

    Air Power_____ 85

CHAPTER 8 _____ 88

    Coordinates_____ 88

    Dealing with Death _____ 91

    The Purple Heart That Wasn't_____ 93

CHAPTER 9 _____ 96

    Heroes_____ 96

    I Thought I Had Trouble _____ 99

    I Stopped My World _____ 102

CHAPTER 10 _____ 106

    Life after Vietnam _____ 106

    Vietnam War _____ 108

GLOSSARY _____ 115

    Locations_____ 115

    Organization of Troop Units_____ 116

    Terms and Abbreviations_____ 117

MAPS

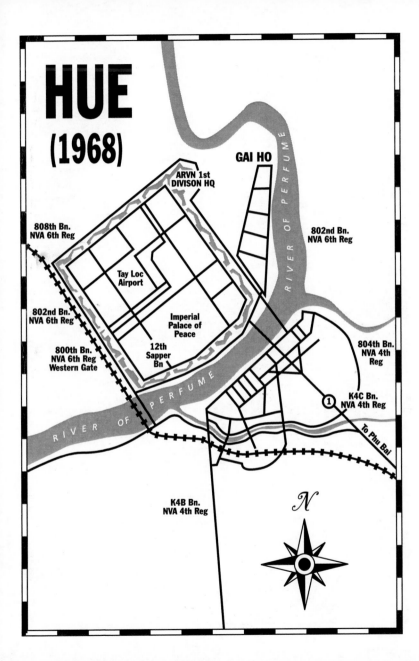

INTRODUCTION

My name is Joseph Walter Babine, and in the 1960s I served in the United States Marine Corps. My tour of duty started with basic training in 1963 at Parris Island, South Carolina, and advanced training at Camp LeJeune in North Carolina. Having made private first class in basic, I got to choose where to go and what to do in the corps. Because I had a desire to go to California, I chose to become a seagoing marine.

After finishing Sea School in San Diego, California, I was assigned to the USS *Chicago*. Since the ship was newly commissioned as a missile cruiser, we had ceremonies that made me a blank owner—that is, one of the first to serve on a newly commissioned ship.

For two years I served as a seagoing marine and then returned a second time to Camp LeJeune. But duty at Camp LeJeune turned out to be just playing war games. Since I really wanted to fight as a marine, I volunteered to go to Vietnam. Although I didn't actually know where Vietnam was, within a month I was on my way to Southeast Asia. In 1966 and 1967 I served in Vietnam with L Company, Third Battalion, 26th Marines.

The stories, opinions, and personal views that you are about to read come from my experience in Vietnam. The stories are true and actually happened to me. Some are interesting, some are tragic, and some are heart-wrenching. Because I lived these experiences, I have always carried them in my mind.

But after Vietnam, as I got caught up in life and work, I did not have time to put them into words. It took me twenty-five years before I started writing about what happened to me in Vietnam. Now, forty-five years have passed since my time in war there. Yet as I write these stories, that past seems like yesterday.

These experiences and stories come from a part of my life that was so dramatic and touched my life so deeply that I can never forget what I lived through and what I encountered there. Writing about my time in Vietnam has helped me come to understand who I am, and in some ways, why I am the person I am today.

CHAPTER 1

GROWING UP

When I was growing up in Maine, I spent a lot of time by myself, though I did not think of myself as a loner. I played a lot of baseball with my cousin Charles, who lived across the field from my grandparents. When my family moved from Maine to Saratoga Springs in upstate New York, however, the transition challenged me. Because the schools in Maine had been so good, I had to adapt to a lower level of skills in my new classes. Since I could always get along with people, school was not a problem. I played baseball, basketball, and football and had one good friend, George Pennimen. Penny and I had a lot in common. We played one-on-one basketball and listened to music. We got together with other kids and had a good time. Penny and I also hitchhiked all around the state, even as far as New York City. Nobody really cared where I was.

When I was thirteen years old, things started to change. My parents separated and eventually divorced.

My mother left us, so my three sisters and I lived with our father. He was a drinker and wasn't around much. I was older than my sisters. Watching out for them, I made sure as best I could that they were okay and that they didn't hang out with the wrong people. Because my sisters were considerably younger than me, they weren't aware of my protection. I would run off the questionable characters and threaten to beat them up if they came back.

During this period of my life, I started to change within myself. I had no one to talk to and didn't want anyone to know what was going on in my life. I thought a lot, worked things out in my own mind, made mistakes, but learned from them. As I entered high school, everyone thought my life was fine. It was not. Although my friend George Pennimen and I never talked about what was going on in my family, he knew. He and I stayed friends all through high school.

While I was in high school, I got a job in a factory working the night shift from eleven at night to seven in the morning. At eight in the morning I went to school. During the summer I kept working at the factory at night, but from nine in the morning to three in the afternoon, I worked as a camp counselor in Saratoga. Then each day from five in the afternoon to nine at night, I worked as a waiter in the famous Wishing Well restaurant. I saw a lot of well-known people there like Edward R. Murrow, President

Eisenhower, the jockeys Willy Shoemaker and Eddie Arcaro, and celebrities. It was fun to see celebrities, but as far as I'm concerned—even now—they are no different than anyone else. So I was not impressed by them. After work in the restaurant, I headed back to the factory. I had no time to do anything else. Now, looking back, I wonder when I slept.

I always got along great with everyone that I worked with. I had a lot of associates as friends, not real close but good people. I grew up fast, but I was strong-minded.

I was not prepared for the deaths in my family. My grandfather passed away and he was followed six months later by my grandmother. I think she died of a broken heart. My aunt Eleanor was already sick when my grandfather was in the hospital. She died not long after my grandmother. I loved the three of them very much.

In 1988 when I was out of the marines and living in California, my father fell ill. He was in the hospital for multiple heath problems. He and my mother had remarried by then. I had medical power of attorney for my father and took care of everything for my mother. I spent two weeks in Saratoga, staying with my mother. My father died shortly afterward. A few years later, my mother also died. But because my family in New York had lost my phone number, I did not know of her death until six months later. Although I was not close to either my mother or my father, their deaths affected me. The loss of my close relatives left a mark on me. I discovered, as so many others have done, that to love someone and lose them is to feel pain.

When I had graduated from high school, I knew I had to leave New York. I was a strong-willed person—self-made—and in very good physical shape. Although all other family members had been in the army, I thought about what I wanted to do and decided that I was ready for the marines.

THE FAMILY PLOT

During my boyhood years in Maine, I used to spend my summers with my grandparents in Brunswick. My grandparents owned a home laundry and would hang the clothes to dry on the lines around the house. I had lots to do in the country area as a ten-year-old boy. I would mow my grandparents' yard every two weeks. I used to get five dimes an acre.

Across the street was a very large cemetery. I liked walking up and down in the cemetery, just looking at the tombstones and reading each one. Sometimes I would take the lawn mower over and mow the grass around the marker and marble tombstones in our family plot. One grave always fascinated me. The name on the tombstone was Walter Raymond and the last name began with B, but I could not pronounce it. I did not recognize the name and wondered who it was. I asked my grandparents and my mother, but no one would talk to me about who was buried there or why.

But there was one person I knew who would tell me. All my young life my aunt Eleanor, one of my mother's three sisters, was good to me. She always told me the truth. If I didn't ask, she wouldn't tell me anything, but if I asked her any direct question, no matter what, she would answer me.

So I questioned her about the grave in the family plot. Aunt Eleanor asked if I really wanted to know. I said yes, and she told me to sit down. The first thing she told me was that it was my brother.

The story she told shocked me. Before my father married my mother, she had already been married. The first marriage did not last, but she had a son. She named him Walter Raymond, after my grandfather Walter. Walter Raymond only lived for six months and then died from pneumonia.

Later my mother married my father, and three years after my brother's death, I was born and given the name Joseph Walter. My first name was my father's, and I always thought I had been given my middle name for my grandfather. But as I found out, I was actually named after my brother. When my cousin Charles was born three months after me, his middle name became Raymond.

Even later in life, when I asked my mother about my brother, she would never talk to me about it. One day, however, without commenting, she handed me the only known picture of my brother Walter Raymond, taken just before he passed away. I was stunned that after twenty years she acknowledged that I actually had had a brother. But to my knowledge, my mother never spoke to anyone about what had happened. It was a family secret, known by everyone, spoken by no one.

Over sixty years have passed, but I still think about that grave in the family plot.

UNITED STATES MARINE CORPS

Leaving home, I went to boot camp in Parris Island, South Carolina. As a teenager who never traveled farther from home than just between Maine and New York, it was interesting to meet men from all over the US in the marines. There were so many different cultures and ways people lived. So many different stories! Of my unit of 120 men in boot camp, only four marines were promoted to PFC. I was one of those four, giving me my choice in assignments. I always wanted to go to California, and by choosing the sea-going marines, I headed off to San Diego.

On the missile cruiser USS *Chicago*, we marines were the security for all the restricted areas. There were only fifty marines to cover the guard stations.

No one, not even the captain, could enter these areas without authorization. We went to interesting places, from San Diego to Long Beach, San Francisco to Puget Sound in Washington, Pearl Harbor in Hawaii to Subic Bay in the Philippines. Our duties didn't allow us to do much. For one thing, we were eight hours on, eight hours off of duty, and confined to the ship, which eliminated the possibility of going anywhere or doing anything that might interest us. Also it seemed like we were always involved in "spit and polish" and keeping up appearances. I did not like my two years as a seagoing marine.

After my seagoing tour was over, I returned to Camp Lejeune in North Carolina where we constantly trained by playing war games. I didn't like to just play so I volunteered to go to the real war in Vietnam. I felt that if I were going to be marine, that's where I should be.

Amazingly, when I got to Southeast Asia, out of thousands of marines, I met up with three friends from seagoing who had come to Vietnam at the same time as I did, though from other places. The four of us stayed in contact in Vietnam.

Adrian Delasandro and Kemp were with the 7th Marines, and Brown and I were with the 3/26th Marines. In Vietnam, both of our units served in the I Zone.

Delasandro, from New York, was a real character—funny and serious—and a great person to be around. But he was also an instigator. One time in Clancy's, a bar in San Francisco, without telling us, he went over to some sailors and told them we didn't like them and were going to beat them up. Then the fight was on. Delasandro, however, had found a table in the back and enjoyed the fight from underneath it. Later, when we found him laughing, we were ready to start a fight with him. He said he hadn't thought we needed him to defend our honor.

In Vietnam, Delasandro was shot and wounded three times. The third time he got a bullet in the groin. He asked the medic how bad he was wounded. The medic, knowing Delasandro's reputation for jokes, told him, "It's a bad place. You'll live, but *it's* gone." That, fortunately for him, wasn't true.

Delasandro was flown to a hospital ship in the Philippines and his recovery took a long time. When I was leaving Vietnam, I stopped in the Philippines to see him. He didn't have to go back to Vietnam because by then he had three Purple Hearts.

Kemp, from Texas, was another great guy— all at once tough and carefree. About five-feet-ten inches tall, he weighed around 200 pounds and was in great shape. Delasandro and he had hung out together a lot. Later when I was down in Hue from the Khe Sanh, I saw Delasandro, and he told me that Kemp had been shot in the chest and killed. Delasandro was very distraught by his friend's death and didn't want to talk about it. During our seagoing days, I too had hung around and worked out with Kemp. His death hit me hard.

Brownie from Tennessee was my closest friend since high school. He was personable. Everyone liked him, and he liked everyone as well. As squad leaders in the Khe Sanh, he as a sergeant and I as a corporal who then became a sergeant, we spent a lot of time together. He enjoyed country western music, as I did. We went to company meetings where we discussed areas of patrol or ambush and areas for company reconnaissance or action. On the base, we talked about Vietnam and about life in general. He talked about Tennessee where he lived and where his family made moonshine in the hills, but they also had a ranch and were well-off. We talked about going into business together and opening a bar.

One day in Quang Tri, we were on patrol, spread out five to ten feet apart to cover the area. Because of the rolling terrain, we couldn't see too far ahead of us. Suddenly, the right side of the platoon was ambushed. The left and middle squads rushed over with support. We defeated the enemy, but everything happened so fast, it wasn't until the fight was over that I realized that Brownie had been killed.

I had never talked about these three friends before I started writing my Vietnam stories. Even today, I feel their loss, and I'll never forget them.

GULF OF TONKIN

Aboard the newly commissioned nuclear missile cruiser USS *Chicago*, I had a two-year tour of duty as a seagoing marine. The main job of the marines was the security of the nuclear ship, encompassing all important areas and stations on board the cruiser. We guarded seven days a week, twenty-four hours a day, and 365 days a year.

During my second year on board, the USS *Chicago* spent about six months in dry dock at Hunters Point in San Francisco, California. Later we traveled to Hawaii, docking at Pearl Harbor for about a month. We then headed to the Philippines at Subic Bay. From there, however, we were not told where we were going.

Leaving Subic Bay we sailed for the South China Sea and entered the Gulf of Tonkin. The Gulf of Tonkin is an arm of the South China Sea, west of Hainan. We had no idea where we were headed, but once we arrived, we found out. We had arrived in Vietnam.

For about a month we patrolled three hundred miles of the north and south coasts bordering Vietnam. We merely cruised back and forth in the

Tonkin Bay but stayed on alert. It seemed ridiculous just to cruise one way then the other. Nothing ever happened.

After our uneventful time in the Tonkin Bay, we traveled back to the Philippines. But when we returned to Subic Bay, we each received medals for—of all things—being in the Vietnam War. A year later, I was on land in Vietnam as a combat marine.

Today I now have two medals for being in Vietnam. Even though I have two, I believe only one of them is real. Twenty years later, from a report about Vietnam issued by the US Government, I found out that at the time we were patrolling the Gulf of Tonkin, the United States had been seriously considering the use of nuclear weapons to eliminate North Vietnam. The USS *Chicago*, a missile cruiser, had been armed with nuclear warheads.

Time and history tell us that the nuclear option was never acted upon. But if a nuclear war had been activated, it would have been launched from the Gulf of Tonkin. As a seagoing marine, I would actually have been *in war* in Vietnam.

CHAPTER 2

AREAS SERVED

In the early years of US involvement in Vietnam—1966–1967—most of the area in the northern section of South Vietnam was controlled by marine units based in the Khe Sanh. I was a part of that combat force.

I spent most of my tour of Vietnam in two regions: the Khe Sanh and Hue. The Khe Sanh, which is neither a city nor a village, was the northernmost US established combat base of South Vietnam. For the NVA it was a key obstacle thrown up at their gateway into South Vietnam from Laos.

In a remote corner of Quang Tri Province, eighteen miles south of the DMZ and North Vietnam and eight miles east of the Laotian border, the Khe Sanh blocked the resupply route of the Ho Chi Minh Trail that came from North Vietnam passing through Laos. The NVA had created an essential supply track that stretched north and south along the borders of

Laos, Cambodia, and North Vietnam, just outside and parallel to the border of South Vietnam.

The entire main US combat base of the Khe Sanh was less than two miles long and one mile wide. The area itself is relatively flat. To the north and west are mountain areas, the western range headed to Laos.

To the north, the mountains rise to a thousand feet and higher. These mountains are very dense and steep with tall trees and large bushes, making foot travel almost impossible. Consequently, this area was mostly patrolled by aircraft.

Bushy with dry grass but close to the Khe Sanh and Laos, the mountain ranges to the west were patrolled all the time. Foot travel and patrols were not difficult in the lower hills.

Highly exposed, the airstrip at the Khe Sanh, however, was extremely dangerous. Instead of concrete, the runway was constructed of crushed compacted rock and multiple steel plates which if damaged, could be removed. The North Vietnamese had their artillery guns and mortars calibrated on the runway in constant bombardment.

Very rarely did any aircraft actually land on this airstrip. Resupply aircraft such as C-123 providers and C-130 cargo planes would skid along the runway—never landing—drop their supplies, and be gone. No resupply plane ever spent more than three minutes before leaving. When they came and left in such a hurry, we could almost hear them saying, "See you later, I'm outta here!"

Because of our air power, the North Vietnamese could not overrun the Khe Sanh. We had support twenty-four hours a day: F-4 Phantoms, F-105 Thunder Chiefs, A-4 Skyhawks and A-6A Intruders. At night B-52 bombers lit up the night as if it were daytime.

Brigadier General Lowell English said, "When you're at the Khe Sanh, you're not really anywhere." I always called the Khe Sanh *the Hell Hole*. The best description I ever heard, however, was from Airman Second Class Allen Belcher. He said, "Being in the Khe Sanh was like sitting in an electric chair and waiting for someone to pull the switch."

Another area where I spent time was Hue, the former Imperial capital of a United Vietnam. Hue is currently the capital of Thua Thien Province. Cut off from the rest of South Vietnam by the Annamese Mountains, Hue was bordered by the DMZ to the north and Laos to the west. Hue lacked any major harbors or ports; the River of Perfume, running east and south and southwest of the city, constituted the only waterway.

Hue is like three different places. In the southwest, it consisted of small houses and huts on unpaved streets, which required house-to-house searches. Outside of this area stretched miles of rice paddies separated by dikes, which were raised dirt paths serving as the only way to walk through the rice fields. West and north, outside of Hue, the terrain changed again. There, valleys and mountain regions were so dense we had to patrol in a single-file line. Although the mountains were not high, they were close together with tall jungle bushes between that we could not penetrate. To get anywhere we had to use trails and paths.

Most of the city's historical strategic and symbolic significance was the northern section of Hue, including the Imperial Citadel. For more than a century, Hue was the center of Vietnamese religious and cultural life. With the Imperial Citadel, known for its pagodas and famous boulevards, Hue was the most exotic city in Vietnam. Over the course of the war, however, the North Vietnamese destroyed Hue, leveling even the Imperial Citadel.

TROUBLE BEFORE TROUBLE

It is ironic that given the trouble I experienced in Vietnam, I almost didn't arrive there. During the previous two years before shipping out for Vietnam, I had been a seagoing marine on the USS *Chicago*, a missile cruiser. Now my unit, the 3/26th Marines, heading to fight in Vietnam, was being transported in a convoy of ships. The USS *Washington*, an aircraft carrier that left from Long Beach, California, carried five thousand of us marines. There I was, crossing the Pacific again.

About five days into our trip, we ran into a tropical storm with hurricane rain and winds. The carrier rocked like a matchstick, and no one was allowed above deck. Waves coming over the ship were at least twenty to thirty feet high. Even below deck we had to man our life jackets. *You have got to be kidding!* I thought. *If this carrier sinks or capsizes, there's no way we'll survive.*

Hanging in rows of hammocks five tiers high, lying on the floor, or trying to stand braced against the bulkheads—we were tossed from side to side. Everyone was seasick. The sounds and smells of vomiting overwhelmed us.

Although I spent two years on the missile cruiser in the Pacific, I had never gotten seasick before. Now here I was, so sick I could hardly move. The huge carrier slammed us back and forth without any pattern, making balance impossible. There was no escape from the continual upheaval; there was literally no place to go.

From the navy personnel rushing by us, we knew our situation was serious but not how serious. We were aware that all the ammunition aboard our ship was in the front. But we did not know that a fire had broken out in that area, and that it was very bad. Furthermore,

JOSEPH W. BABINE

we had no way of knowing what was going on with the other four or five ships in our convoy.

Twenty-four hours later, the storm was finally over. When we went above deck, we saw how bad it had been. Armored personnel vehicles and tanks that had been tied on the decks were no longer there—just gone. Two of the ships in the convoy were badly damaged, with twisted parts of superstructures and decks stripped bare. In spite of the significant damage, the ships were capable of moving on. So we continued toward Vietnam. It was trouble before trouble.

THE LANDING

When about 2,500 of us marines were deployed to Vietnam, although we knew where we were going, no one ever told us where we were or the route we were taking to get there. It took about two months to cross the Pacific on the USS *Washington*, an old aircraft carrier refitted for troop transport. Surviving a tropical storm, we proceeded to the South China Sea and then to the Gulf of Tonkin. Our two marine battalions would actually be the first American combat troops in Vietnam.

A couple of miles out from our destination, Amtraks were waiting for us. The Amtrak, a flat-bottomed, armed military vehicle equipped with both tracks and rudder, could travel on land or in water. It was used chiefly for landing assault troops. We

35

were then told we were going to make an amphibious landing. The only thing I knew about amphibious landings was what I had seen in World War II films. We had never trained for such a landing, but we were ready for whatever we had to do.

Boarding the Amtraks about a half mile off the coast, we approached the shoreline in a place known as Da Nang, a seaport formerly called Tourane by the French.

After the Amtraks churned through calm waters to reach the coast, the front gates of the vessels slammed open, each disgorging about a hundred marines carrying all their gear to surge forward in the surf and sand toward the shoreline. In all, thousands of men stormed the sands of Da Nang. Not knowing what would be waiting for us, we hit the beach battle-ready. But once we landed on the beach front, which was a long strip of sand leading up to a solid line of trees, we saw that we were the only ones lined up the whole length of the shore. No one else was there.

Suddenly, from the trees emerged a group of twenty to thirty Vietnamese women moving toward us. They wore loose black robes and round straw hats. To us, they all looked the same with Asian features like the women in the Philippines. Although the women were small of stature, when we saw them later walking rhythmically with poled burdens balanced across their shoulders, we realized how strong they were.

We were stunned and speechless. There we were, ready to fight a war, when the women began placing wreaths of flowers around our necks and welcoming us to their country! Although we knew we were in war, the women's peaceful approach was a shocking welcome.

Leaving the beach, we found the town of Da Nang right behind the trees. There we boarded trucks and convoyed to a place called Hue. That was where our war started.

Just outside of the city to the west, we started setting up a base. On a slight elevation my company was digging fox holes. About 200-300 meters away, the mortar company was setting up their equipment. Suddenly word spread like wild fire: a marine had been killed by a single sniper shot. His name was Edwards, a big guy over six-feet tall. Even though I didn't personally know him, I knew him by sight. When we heard he was dead, we realized we were no longer in a game—death had become a reality. It put us on alert. From then on, for us, our first base was known as Camp Edwards, named after that first marine killed there.

In the next few years, the base at Hue, which started out with us first twenty-five hundred marines, expanded into a huge installation. It developed like a small city with over twenty-five thousand marines. Although I entered Vietnam in Da Nang, I never saw that coast again until I left.

CHAPTER 3

WHAT GOES AROUND
COMES AROUND

When I was a young marine corporal— only eighteen years old—and getting advanced training in Camp LeJeune, North Carolina, I had a sergeant who was cocky, arrogant, self-centered, and a know-it-all. Although he was in charge, he himself was young and did not know how to handle people or authority.

It seemed this sergeant did not like me at all. I was a strong-willed person, and I believe that was threatening to him. Our personalities conflicted, but I kept my mouth shut and did what I was told. Some assignments he gave me were uncalled for. The camp boasted old WWII quonset huts sometimes used for storage or even personnel. So one time, he had me guarding an abandoned one: nobody around or in it. Another time he sent me to "guard" one of the infamous swamps which posed no threat unless an unlucky patrol sent there for a two a.m. exercise encountered

JOSEPH W. BABINE

alligators or deep water. Instead of assigning a unit to clean toilets, he made me clean them alone. One petty harassment followed another.

Because his attitude was wrong, I felt confident that I was a better marine and a better person than that sergeant. Nevertheless, he was in charge. Two years later, however, in an area known as the Khe Sanh in Vietnam, I was promoted from corporal to sergeant. At times, the Khe Sanh resembled a revolving door. Marines were transferred or wounded, or at the end of their tour of duty or they were killed.

After I was in the Khe Sanh about six months, a new fellow transferred into our company. Lo and behold, it was the former sergeant who had tormented me in North Carolina. By the time he arrived at the Khe Sanh, he had been demoted from sergeant to corporal. I didn't know why and, personally, I didn't care. But I suspected his arrogance had something to do with it. Now, two-and-a-half years after Camp LeJeune, I was the sergeant in charge of his platoon.

Although we recognized each other, we said nothing. But we both anticipated a follow up to the Camp LeJeune antagonism. The new corporal realized that his misuse of authority in the past had him now headed for trouble. The look in his eyes gave him away. He and I knew I was in a position to get even for the way he treated me before.

But I didn't know what I wanted to do, so time went by. I started to see he was disturbed by my not doing anything. His expressions were wary—more paranoid—waiting for something to happen. I decided that not doing anything was a good way to handle the situation. I treated the corporal as I did all the other marines who were following orders and doing their job in Vietnam. By not lowering myself to the arrogant level of the other person—not taking revenge— I realized the other person suffered more mentally.

If a person wants revenge, it is valuable to think twice before acting. In some cases, doing nothing is the answer. It can make one a stronger and better person, which will be noticed by others. For me, this encounter at a young age was a major learning experience in life and something I have never forgotten.

When the corporal and I came back to the United States from Vietnam, we were released from the Marine Corps at the same time at El Toro, California. I shook his hand, and he wished me well, then added, "Thank you." Both of us had learned a lesson in life: What goes around comes around.

THE CARDS

During my time in Vietnam, I was promoted to company platoon sergeant in a place called Hue. We had been there a few months at Camp, where we'd had a few new Marines join the platoon and company.

From Hue we moved north to a place called the Khe Sanh near the border of North Vietnam and Laos. As far as I was concerned the Khe Sanh was a hell hole.

When we arrived, a combat base had already been established. We were a part of the expansion; on the west end we dug new trenches and used sand bags for fortification. One day while I was walking our perimeter and checking my platoon, I noticed a new young marine playing with a deck of cards on the sand bags. He told me he was Private Williams from Tennessee. Curious, I asked Williams what he was doing with the cards. He was reading them, he said. I thought that reading cards must be a game that I had never seen before. In fact, I had never seen cards like the ones he was using. They were bigger and more colorful than the usual playing deck. The private told me that these were tarot cards that could tell the past and future.

I couldn't believe what I was hearing. "OK," I told Williams, "read the cards to me." I knew for a fact that I had never met Williams before nor had he met me. He started turning over the tarot cards. As he read them to me, he told me that I had three younger sisters and a brother who had died before I was born and that my parents had a problem with drinking and had separated because of it.

How could he have known all these truths about me through a deck of cards? But he was not finished. He told me that although I would have a bad time in

Vietnam and a hard time getting out of there, I would make it. I felt it was crazy for him to say this.

"Okay," I said. "If I'm going to make it out of here, what's going to happen to you?"

He turned over the cards for himself and told me, "It still comes out the same."

"What do you mean?" I asked. The young man told me that he himself would not make it out of Vietnam. He didn't say much more. It seemed like he was in a trance. His body still, his eyes fixed on the cards, his voice with the same low trancelike conviction, he said, simply, "I will not make it out of VietNam." He was always very quiet and stayed within himself. Following orders, doing his job, and being where he was supposed to be, Williams was a good marine. Since I was his platoon sergeant, I told Williams that I would do everything I could to see that he would make it out of Vietnam. I determined I would keep him close to me and always know where he was.

Six months later, we were still at the Khe Sanh, and the situation was bad. But I have to say, I never looked after a person as I did Williams. I wasn't sure how much I believed in his cards, but I worried about the possibility of him getting killed. I had a lot of other marines and responsibility, but I watched over Williams the best I could. I couldn't leave him at the base; I couldn't risk others shielding him. But I made sure he wasn't alone or unnecessarily exposed. I never made him a point man or a squad leader.

I didn't want to buy his story that he would die. I wanted him to survive, to prove that the cards were wrong about his death. As for my fate, I just knew that whatever was going to happen to me was going to happen. If I had believed what the cards said about me, it could have made me less aggressive, less careful, and less controlled as a fighter.

One afternoon while on patrol, we ran into an ambush atop a hill 861. I knew where Williams was—right in the middle of the squad. We stormed the hill to overtake the enemy. Looking to my left only twenty feet away, I could not believe what I saw. Williams was shot in the chest and killed. Just like that! Gone! Dodging enemy fire, I ran to him, picked him up by the flight jacket and yelled, "No, don't do this to me!" I was angry, tears coming to my eyes. I felt so powerless: I had been unable to prevent his prediction of his death from coming true. Yes, we took the hill. And, yes, I was wounded too. I had a hard time. But Williams didn't make it.

I had never heard of or seen tarot cards before I met Private Williams. I have never seen tarot cards since. I can't say that I don't believe in the cards or in palm reading or in other occult sources of information. I myself don't use them, but I leave open their possibilities for others. I owe my open mind to a very good marine and good man that read his cards to me.

THE TRAIL

In the northern region of Vietnam where only marines were stationed, we were always out on day patrols and night ambushes. The North Vietnamese used Laos as a resupply route to South Vietnam, a route known as the Ho Chi Minh Trail.

One day after the rainy season, the ground was already drying up in the thin altitude, but the intensive heat of the summer hadn't hit yet. Our unit had plans for a special reconnaissance to an area west of the Khe Sanh; this patrol would take us into Laos. led a small force of thirty men, four of whom were from a demolition crew. Having such a small group for the reconnaissance, our mission was not to engage but to gain information for future ground force and air strikes.

Being the sergeant in charge, I usually assigned a point man as scout. On this patrol, however, personally knowing the terrain well and what to look for, I decided—as I often did—to lead the patrol myself and take the point. As we left the bushy down slope from Vietnam, we entered Laos following one of the many trails through over grown brush and bunched copses of tall trees scrabbling at the blue sky over our heads. Although the terrain was difficult, there were trails. We followed them but were forced by the density of vegetation to travel one behind the other on the hard beaten surface the narrow foot paths.

I was in the lead, moving very slowly, looking for signs of travel or booby traps—had the earth been moved or branches broken or foliage out of place? Were leaves too neatly placed? Were there trip wires? If a hole had been dug, the soil would have been shifted on to the side of the trail. So, not only did the point man have to watch the trail, but it was very important to watch the sides as well.

Approaching the Ho Chi Minh Trail, I started to find the booby traps. In a two hundred yard straightway, I located eleven traps. A few were punji traps—holes dug 18x18 inches with very hard bamboo shoots, sharpened and set at an angle to go through the ankle, more often than not tipped with poison. Leaves would cover the pit. Trip wires laid across the trail were ready to set off slingshot-type devices like boards with spikes or sharpened objects to injure or kill. I saw empty c-ration cans that people liked to pick up or kick, but these had hand grenades in them with the pins pulled, ready to explode.

As I was looking down the trail and to the sides, I stepped on a strange configuration of leaves. I heard a puff. I knew I had stepped on a pressurized device. I also knew that if I lifted my foot, the booby trap would explode.

I stood, frozen, and called the demolition crew. "Don't move!" they cautioned me. Using a knife, they dug out the dirt around my foot and around the device. It was a three-pronged pressurized green canister that could only be disarmed from the top. But my foot was on that top. If I lifted my foot, the device would blow up.

Because the canister would explode in a 360 degree arc, up and out for about 100 meters, the demolition crew moved everyone back hundreds of yards. They told me to jump straight out and low and face first. "That way you'll probably only lose a foot or leg." I wanted to know if this was the only way. They said it was.

I had my flight jacket on and the demolition guy took his jacket and two others and wrapped them around my foot and leg. Then they walked away, leaving me standing there.

"Where are you going?" I called after them. The demolition engineer turned around with a knowing grin, "You don't think we're going to stay next to you, do you?" It was amazing how quiet and calm everything was.

There I was all by myself, and I began to sweat. My life flashed before me, and I have to say it didn't take long. I saw myself as a young child, as a high school kid, and as a marine. I realized I hadn't even lived yet.

JOSEPH W. BABINE

Although only minutes had passed, it seemed like I was alone there for a long, long time. Over and over I planned my dive, not wanting to do it. But I had to. There was no other way, just jump out fast and low. I couldn't think about it anymore. *Well*, I decided, *it's better to lose a part of myself than my life.*

I bent my knees, leaned forward, and pushed with the foot that was on the canister. I jumped, head first and low, for as far as I could. Then I heard only a puff. The canister I had been standing on was a dud. A wave of shock passed through me. Relief set in as I gathered myself from the ground, standing on the legs that I had only moments before said my good-byes to.

To this day, every time I walk down a path or trail, I find myself instinctively looking at the ground and what is lining the sides. I think back about the trail I walked down those many years ago.

THE HILL

In the northern region of South Vietnam is an area known as the Khe Sanh, or the I Zone. When I served there from 1966-1967, it was a marine-oriented zone, dominated by "Conventional Warfare." The NVA we faced were as well-equipped as we were, with high quality assault weapons.

Later, after I had left Vietnam, things changed at the Khe Sanh. From 1967-1968, General

Westmoreland, ordering that the Khe Sanh be held at any cost, brought in thousands of Special Forces and army cavalry units as well more marines to reinforce the Khe Sanh and hold it.

In my time, five to ten patrols went out every day and a similar number of ambushes were set every night. The day patrols were for reconnaissance to survey and gain information about enemy territory. Night ambushes were sent to predetermined locations. To set up ambushes off paths, trails, hills or rivers known to be used by the NVA, the twenty or so men on the ambush would be strategically placed depending on the terrain. Always, however, all sides would be covered. Out in front of us, we would set up claymore mines designed to produce a directed fan-shape pattern of fragments. Although the ambushes could be effective, I felt they made us sitting ducks. There we sat, watching deep darkness, our eyes ready to play tricks on us, quiet enough to hear the slightest rustle in the brush, wondering whose target we were: it was almost enough to drive me crazy.

West of the Khe Sanh, three mountain ranges saddled each other. The mountains were designated 861A, 861, and 881S. The numbers relate to the elevations of the range. All three were bushy with high dry grass and very few trees. Mountain Range 861 became the scene of chaos and death.

One particular day, my platoon was patrolling west of the Khe Sanh and east of Laos. During our reconnaissance we crossed over all three of the ranges and went into the valley. Nothing happened on the patrol; it was easy. In late afternoon when we came back to our home base in the Khe Sanh, the lieutenant gathered me and the squad leaders, as we always did, to critique the patrol we were just on. As we were discussing and evaluating the area and terrain for future patrols, we received a surprising report from air reconnaissance: a large North Vietnamese force had been spotted on Hill 861. We had just crossed over that mountain a few hours before. With that news, we shook our heads and rolled our eyes—no panic.

Immediately following the air report, we received orders directing us to return to the hill and secure it before nightfall. We grabbed our gear and our men and crossed our base to the helicopter pad where the Chinooks capable of carrying twelve tons of supplies and troops were ready to transport us. Before we arrived at the hill, we called in air strikes to bomb the area. The jets were dropping two hundred and fifty pound bombs, along with bombs containing napalm, a highly incendiary jelly-like substance used in fire bombs fire bombs which scorched the earth leaving a landscape blackened and devoid of any sign of life.

When the helicopter I was riding in was twenty-five feet from landing, we could hear pinging sounds from enemy fire hitting the helicopter. We were in a free-fall the last twenty-five feet. The impact rattled my teeth and shook my bones, but we were okay to continue. As we climbed out of the helicopter, I directed my men to the bottom of the hill.

Two other helicopters landed, one to our left and one to our right. We were in the middle, thus forming a perimeter.

We mobilized to the bottom of 861 and began to go up the hill on line. We were shooting up hill at a disadvantage. The return fire intensified as we started up. Hitting the ground, we checked out the positions of the enemy fire. Not only were they using assault weapons, but they were throwing hand grenades.

Going up the hill was not a track meet. Under fire and climbing, each marine lugged a minimum of sixty pounds of supplies. This included backpacks with extra ammunition, cartridge belts with at least six double magazines of ammo for rifles, four to six canteens of water, extra pouches of hand grenades, and wearing a twenty-pound flight jacket as well. We stayed as low as we could, and kept moving upward.

Our Captain, from Long Beach, new to the Khe Sanh but arrogant from previous marine experience, must have fancied himself another Audie Murphy. He rushed to the front of everyone to lead the charge up the hill. About halfway up, he caught a bullet in the neck. When the medic used a knife to open the wound, he found that the captain's jugular vein had been severed. The medic reached his hand in to pinch the vein to try to stop the blood from spurting out. A chopper was ready to MedEvac the captain, but he didn't last long enough to see it. He never made it off the hill. He was neither the first nor the last to die around me.

Of the marines climbing the sides of the hill, my men and I were under the heaviest fire. Bullets and grenades rained down on us. Our machine gun squad always worked to coordinate with us. They knew their job and wanted to be sure that their positions effectively supported us. I was familiar with McDonald, a kid from San Bernardino, often talking to him about the placement of his machine gun squad. He was behind me when I heard others shouting. I turned around to see McDonald, as well as Private Willlams, shot and killed.

About three-fourths of the way up the hill, my radioman, Wallace from Texas, was on my right, just a little in front of me. As he turned to his left, a bullet hit the radio on his back and deflected toward me, hitting me in the back of the neck. I hit the ground. I reacted to the stinging in my neck and pulled my hand away covered with blood. My wound was superficial, so I continued up the hill. I bent over low and close to the ground, aware of the fast-changing conditions.

THE DARK SHADOWS OF VIETNAM

Just before I reached the top, with a renewal of heavy firing, I hit the ground again as a grenade struck my right hand, shredding it with hot shrapnel. I shifted my rifle to my left hand and continued.

As we reached the top, the second column was filling in behind us. Of our column, only two out of seventeen were still alive, and both of us were wounded. With the convergence of all our squads at the top, we had secured Hill 861 by nightfall, as we had been ordered to do. But not without a heavy price.

We had patrolled the range earlier that day. So the question was: How did the North Vietnamese get there so fast?

We found that just off the center of the hill about twenty feet down the slope, the NVA had dug out a cave that they accessed from the top by ladder. Tunnels, which could house at least seventy men along with their supplies, spidered out from the cave area. The area, so well camouflaged to the natural terrain, could not be seen. Nothing looked out of place. The answer to our question was chilling: the Vietnamese had been there when we had patrolled.

——————

It must have been a Chinook that evacuated me to Hue. I don't remember clearly. After about a month for recovery, I was returned—of all places—to the Khe Sanh where more hell continued.

To this day I can't help thinking about what happened on Hill 861. In my hand I still have shrapnel that could not be removed. In cold weather my hand and fingers go numb.

During my recovery-period in Hue, I had time to think about what I had gone through. The worst part was remembering the marines I served with who were killed on The Hill. As for what happened to me personally, I got shot down in a helicopter deflected a bullet that hit me in the neck and had my hand torn by a grenade. Meanwhile, all around me Marines were being killed.

For me, the whole experience of Hill 861 was very complex. In the middle of the battle, I could only concentrate on fighting and getting up the hill. Later, as I thought about my individual experiences: getting shot down, being wounded in the neck and finally having my hand shredded by shrapnel, I was stunned by the reality of what had happened specifically to me. Meanwhile, both on the hill and later in the hospital, I could not forget all those Marines who had been dying around me.

You could say I had a bad day.

CHAPTER 4

NINE HUNDRED KILLED

In a convoy on the only main highway from Hue, our marine company was returning to the Khe Sanh. We were near Quang Tri when from a bare hill on our right, about a half mile away, a wave of North Vietnamese barreled toward us, screaming and hollering and firing their weapons.

From that distance carrying only Russian AK-47s, they were too far away to hit us. We threw ourselves to the ground on the side of the road and waited for them to get close enough so we could shoot. We called in air strikes from the Khe Sanh. Within minutes, the jets arrived, six planes dropping bombs and napalm. Within a half-hour, the North Vietnamese were wiped out, their bodies littering the hillside.

During the attack we wondered how they could be so crazy. But later, we found marijuana and other drugs in their gear that must have accounted for their insane assault. Where the enemy came from or what they were doing before they attacked us, we never knew. To me, the whole assault was bizarre, crazy as a rock concert, maniacs out of control.

Our convoy continued to the Khe Sanh. Within hours of our arrival, we received a casualty report from the cleanup company. The confirmed body count reported nine hundred North Vietnamese killed. And we hadn't fired a single shot.

MIRACLE HIT

One day my squad was patrolling a hill through terrain thick with vines, bushes, and trees growing trunk to trunk. We walked single-file on the only trail.

At the top of the upslope of the hill we came to a sharp turn. As our point man approached the turn, a machine gun with the *tut-tut-tut-tut* blast of a Chinese-made weapon opened fire. The force of the bullets smashed the point marine so hard it sent him flying backward down the hill past about five marines, including myself. Immediately we opened fire, destroying the machine-gun nest and killing the two enemy shooters who had been at the corner of the trail right in front of us.

Our point man had been hit at least ten times. All ten rounds hit directly on his body. His helmet, magazine cartridge, flight jacket, and cartridge belt were riddled with bullet holes. The force of the powerful blast convinced him that he was going to die. Our medic rushed to the marine's side and ripped off the man's body coverings to get to the wounds.

Miraculously, however, not one bullet had actually penetrated his body. What he felt oozing and had thought was blood was, in fact, water flowing from his bullet-riddled canteens

Although he was in severe shock and had to be flown out by helicopter, he lived. One thing for sure, though, neither he nor we will ever forget that miracle hit.

ONE-MAN PATROLS

In my time in Vietnam, setting up night ambushes with teams of at least thirty-five to forty marines happened frequently; the marine corps does not recommend nor even train anyone to do one-man patrols. As leader of our ambush team, I received my orders from my lieutenant. Those orders came to him from the captain who received them from our commanding officer. After I got my orders, I would set up meetings with my squad leaders before we left camp, using maps to plan our ambush.

Being a sergeant and because I had already been on numerous patrols, I knew a lot about the area and terrain of Vietnam. On each ambush I had the key challenge of accurately reading the maps in the incredible dark of the night.

For some areas, if we didn't have enough men, we simply wouldn't go. For instance, we would never go on the Ho Chi Minh Trail in Laos or into the northern circle of mountains where we knew there were at least 750,000 NVA. However, I could not stand to sit and wait for the enemy to come to me. Every time I got our ambush set up, I would tell my radioman, "When headquarters calls, tell them I'm down the line." Then I would head out on my one-man reconnaissance patrol.

One night, outside of Hue, I received orders for an ambush. I had three squads, and we were to set up the ambush on a trail leading into the city. Parallel to a wide river, the trail had flattened out from extensive passing of rice paddy farmers. In a heavily wooded area behind the river path, we set up our position to ambush anyone coming or going on the trail.

Once we established our ambush position, I set out along the trail on my usual one-man patrol. Going off the path was no option as it would make too much noise that could be heard by the enemy. My progress was slow. After walking for miles, I came across a fork in the footpath and continued down a new trail that was wider than the one I had been using. Early that morning it had been raining and puddles of water potted the trail. After I traveled a distance, I stopped and recognized that I was in Laos. In actuality, I was traversing the Ho Chi Minh Trail itself, the main supply route for the North Vietnamese.

Proceeding a while longer, I realized I was moving too far away from my squads at the ambush site. Noticing a small knoll above the trail, I stretched out flat on top of it to listen. Then I heard troops approaching. I had to be very still and quiet.

As the NVA passed below me, I started counting them. When I got to four thousand, I stopped. My pulse raced; I tried not to breathe loudly. Hidden only five feet away from a huge enemy force, my insides tightened. I felt I wasn't getting enough air, but I was too scared to make noise by breathing any harder.

Once they had passed, I waited at least an hour before I left the knoll. But from this one-man patrol, I was able to make a full report and, using maps, able to pinpoint the area. Later that week, B-52 bombers totally obliterated that section of the trail.

Another time in Hue, we received orders for a night ambush. As usual, I met with my squad leaders to set a plan, and we proceeded to our ambush site outside of the city. For walking the rice paddies around Hue, there were raised levees above the water. So, on my customary one-man patrol, I walked on the sloped side of the levee to avoid being seen. After traveling for about a mile, I came to a bridge at the end of the paddies. Below, a river moved rapidly and very large lily pads floated quickly with the current.

The lily pads were up to six feet in diameter. I suspected that by using bamboo sticks to breathe, the enemy could possibly be traveling under those pads. Setting myself on the corner down slope of the bridge ready to shoot, I started to throw rocks. I spent at least two hours throwing rocks at the lily pads, hoping to force the possibly unseen enemy to come up to the surface. Much later, however, when I told this story, people laughed. "You're in a war," they joked. "And you're throwing rocks!" When I started to think about it, I guess it was funny. But at the time it was very serious.

But my solo patrols did not happen without problems. At one point, the lieutenant asked me why, whenever I went on an ambush, he could never get hold of me. He questioned my radioman and squad leader about what I was doing.

Discovering my tactic, the lieutenant informed the captain and the captain called me in. "What in the world do you think you're doing?" he demanded. "You're in charge, and you're putting your men in danger!"

I told the captain straight out that it was totally the opposite. First, I had to know for myself and for my men whether any threat was out there. Furthermore, night patrols with a number of people make too much noise. But alone on my scouting patrol, I could investigate the area without being heard. I assured him that my one-man patrols were for reconnaissance, not for engaging the enemy.

After this encounter did I continue to make one-man patrols? Yes, and I never heard about it again, neither from the lieutenant nor the captain.

CHAPTER 5

LANG VEI

A hilltop known as Lang Vei, in the northwest corner of the densely wooded area of the Quang Tri Province, served as an observation post for the I Corps Tactical Zone. Very rugged terrain separated Lang Vei, located 4.5 miles southwest of the Khe Sanh, from our combat base.

The observation post was just off the major Route 9 and 1.5 miles from the Laotian border. Lang Vei, originally the name of a nearby village, perched on a high cliff rising out of the extremely rough terrain contiguous with the Khe Sanh. It overlooked a vast area of Laos to the southwest, providing security information for the marines in the Khe Sanh.

The US Army Green Berets were assigned the Lang Vei observation post. Although they had access to marine and air strike support, they managed to get overrun at night, not once but twice in one month. Each time, we marines from the Khe Sanh had to go to recover the outpost. We resented having to bail them out because it stretched us thin in our own area.

At night there was no way we could cover the 4.5 miles of rugged terrain on foot and be there in time to repulse the attacks. So even though we secured the post, the job wasn't finished until the next morning. By the second attack, most of the Army Green Berets had been wounded or killed. When the Army Special Forces left the observation post after the second time they were overrun, they didn't come back.

We marines took over the location and stabilized the area with radio contact, support from units in the area, and air support. Eventually Special Forces did send a much larger unit to take over the observation post, freeing us again to get on with fighting the NVA.

This time, the returned Special Forces followed our recommendations, securing the post the way it should have been done. They set up a barbed wire fenced perimeter studded with claymore mines. The command post and tank support were situated in the middle of the base. Mortars were set up, and small units strategically circled the perimeter. Trenches were dug to surround the hill, and .50 caliber machine guns were put in place. The base expanded significantly, as needed in that vulnerable area.

When the Green Berets had initially arrived at Lang Vei, I questioned why they were there and what they were supposed to do. Lacking sufficient personnel and defenses for the location, the base was seriously inadequate. It was obvious that the Special Forces were unprepared to establish an observation outpost. They did not know what to do. They should not have been there.

After my experience with the Green Berets in Lang Vei, it may seem that I have no respect for them, which is not altogether true. I'm sure they usually do a good job in what they do. But I just do not know what that objective was. From experience, however, I do not want them looking out for me. Even on an observation post.

INSPECTION OF PERIMETER

During many of the nights after patrol in Vietnam, we set up our night perimeter base—usually on higher ground. One particular night, I dispersed my men on the northwest side of a hill that was covered with heavy vegetation and boulders, and we settled in. Later in the night, I began my inspection of the perimeter. I used my inspection as a reconnaissance to make sure the men were awake and alert. Approaching another marine necessitated a code word to identify persons as friendly. Because the men were spaced far apart, I moved slowly and quietly, so they would not know I was there.

In a five-foot crevice between two tall rocks with only one way in or out, a young marine had fallen

THE DARK SHADOWS OF VIETNAM

asleep. Moving slowly, I took his rifle and started to withdraw. About ten feet away I stopped. I realized that taking his weapon was not a very smart move. What if we were attacked and this young man, with nothing to defend himself, got killed?

I returned to where the marine lay sleeping. But this time I was not quiet. I deliberately made noise and startled him awake. As he instinctively reached for his rifle, he found it was gone and began to shake, his eyes wide with nervous confusion. As I handed him his rifle, I reminded him, "We're not in a game. You could be killed." Then, leaving to continue my inspection, I calmly tapped him on the arm and told him, "Just stay awake."

Two lessons emerged from this experience—one for the young man and another for me. The young man turned out to be a very responsible marine and in time became one of my squad leaders. As for me, I realized that it was more important as a leader to teach others about the right way of doing things than to try being clever.

HOT AND COLD

Of all the places I have been in my life, Vietnam was both the hottest and coldest I have ever experienced. In the Khe Sanh, where we patrolled daily, the jungle was thick, and the open area covered over with eight to ten-feet-tall suffocating elephant grass that made breathing difficult.

During patrols in the summer months when the temperature easily reached 120 degrees, we carried sixty pounds of equipment and sometimes more. Although each marine had at least six canteens of water, sometimes that wasn't enough. But people reacted differently to the heat. Guys from states where they experienced hot temperatures often felt at home in the sweltering weather. But a guy who was raised in a colder region could pass out from heatstroke and dehydration. Invariably, this would start a chain reaction among other men unused to such extreme temperatures. We would have to call back to base for a helicopter. Then we had to carry them out to a secure landing zone from where they could be MedEvaced out.

To counter the heat and to save the number of troops we had, we changed all our patrols to night patrols. But night patrols moved slower because of darkness. Noise was the biggest threat. Given the intense echo of each small noise, large numbers of moving men in the dark was dangerous, because it could alert the enemy to our position. The scraping of equipment against the tress, the moving through brush along the trail, the crunching of boot steps on the path—all these produced magnified sounds in the blackness of the night. There could be no talking at all. Everything was done in hand signals, made doubly difficult because of the darkness. However, in spite of the dangers inherent in the night, the temperature fell into the tolerable nineties, eliminating heatstroke and making the patrols in the night bearable.

During the monsoon season in the Khe Sanh, we were sent on extended reconnaissance to areas where we hoped to engage the enemy. Miles away from base for the two weeks or so that we were gone, all we had was what we carried on our backs during our patrol. Any resupplies had to be dropped five miles from our actual location in order to keep our position hidden from the enemy.

Although we paid no attention to dates or calendars, as the months we call winter—December, January, February—arrived, the rains began. Falling slowly at first, they built into the continuous, ravaging downpours of the monsoon. With the rains came a bitter cold that was intensified by relentless freezing winds. It rained continually for forty straight days and nights; the air was frigid, the winds piecing.

On one such patrol, we came upon an abandoned French fortress that had been constructed in the fifties when they were fighting and losing against the conventional North Vietnamese Army. When we found the installation, vegetation had smothered it. But the defense system impressed us with the depth and width of its trenches that surrounded the massive hill. A man could stand in one of the trenches and not see over the top.

We stayed there for two miserable days. It rained so intensely that I could not see my hand in front of my face. My teeth chattered, and my ribs hurt constantly from the rigid tenseness of my body trying to keep warm.

Even worse, when we had to go to the bathroom, we would freeze if we removed any piece of clothing. So we just went inside our already wet uniforms. Leeches sucked on every part of our bodies. Even though we wore boots and strapped our pants tightly to our legs, they got inside our clothes and attached to our flesh. Small, about two inches long when they started, they swelled up to around four or six inches with the blood they sucked. But the only way to know they were there was to keep checking. At one point, I had to spend a month in Hue to recover from the leeches that had fastened on my legs—from my thighs to my feet.

Although I was born in Maine, I was never so cold in all my life as on those patrols. Considering, then, both the extreme heat and then intense cold of the Khe Sanh, I have never been so terribly hot or as bitterly frozen anywhere in my own country as I was in Vietnam.

THE DARK SHADOWS OF VIETNAM

CHAPTER 6

FRAGGING

In the period between 1965-1970, the US Army and the US Marine Corps defined fragging as slang meaning to kill, wound, or assault a fellow soldier or marine.

In different situations in Vietnam when sending men on patrol, it was very important that there were the right number of troops for that area. A squad, for example, was the smallest unit, consisting of about twelve or thirteen men, while a platoon comprised three squads or more and a company combined two or more platoons.

In the Khe Sanh, the NVA had hundreds of thousands more conventional warfare troops than the Viet Cong in Hue. The VC were guerrilla fighters and snipers but were generously supplied by the NVA who wanted to prevent the guerrillas from defecting to the south.

Given the enormous number of enemy troops in and surrounding the Khe Sanh, a small squad should never have gone on patrol. A squad doesn't stand a chance because they will always confront large numbers of NVA. Those twelve or thirteen marines of the squad would be right out shot and killed. Therefore, in the Khe Sanh, a wise leader made sure that a platoon— and more often a company— patrolled the area. On the other hand, Hue, an area different in terrain and warfare, smaller reconnaissance units could patrol and survey locales to gain information.

After being in Vietnam for a year as platoon sergeant, I knew Hue and the Khe Sanh very well. I knew the trails, I knew the hills, and I knew every detail on the map. Likewise, I knew my men. Marines came into the field without experience. Those new men were assigned to the third squad. The seasoned marines of the first squad were the spearhead of an engagement and were followed by the next two squads with lesser degrees of experience. Spending a great deal of time with my squad leaders, both in action and in the debriefings after each patrol, I knew my men well. These squad leaders, in turn, knew their individual men equally well.

Men functioned better in one situation rather than another. For instance, one man was capable of directly plunging in and taking out a machine gun nest. Another knew how to seal off emotion when dealing with the death of a fellow marine. Someone else could unhesitatingly provide cover for a squad under fire. Yet, another guy understood how to flank correctly to get behind a sniper. One marine might be a natural leader heading up a hill, and others seeing him take point, less afraid now than when being in front of the line, would courageously follow that leader. We had to count on other people to look out for each other. Basically, we had to work together as a unit.

Superior to me, a lieutenant issued my orders for the patrols or ambushes. During my tour, I had had good relationships with a number of lieutenants. They were professional marines who kept close tabs on the situations in the field. We worked together effectively because we operated with mutual trust and communication.

On one occasion, however, a lieutenant was transferred out, and a new lieutenant replaced him. Right out of officers' school, the new lieutenant gave the impression that he knew everything. He went by what he thought the books on war taught. He thought war was tactical, like WWII: moving troops around to gain territory. That was not Vietnam, a situation that required near-at-hand analysis of specific terrain and threat followed by a tactic to address it.

While the new lieutenant knew nothing about Vietnam, he knew even less about how to handle people. He expected men to follow orders like puppets, and he never listened to them to learn from their experiences. He ignored the advice of the men who had been working the Khe Sanh for months and who were uncomfortably aware of the huge number of enemy troops that traveled constantly in the area. He had no idea of the geographic proximity of Laos or the Ho Chi Minh trail nor an understanding of the NVA's strategy to engage only with smaller forces. One time, for instance, his orders directed us off Route 9 that headed toward Laos. We would have ended up with a small number of men right on the Ho Chi Minh trail like sitting ducks for the enemy.

Giving orders for patrols to the west, east, and south, he insisted on sending squads where platoons should go. As a result, our smaller units were being ambushed by large enemy forces, and marines were being killed. At least five or six times, going out in a squad of thirteen, the men failed to return by the morning. This required sending out a platoon to search for the missing unit only to find them all dead, right where the Lieutenant had ordered them to go. Nevertheless, his reaction to the concern of his sergeants and men was "I'm in charge and everyone under my command will do things my way!"

As more troops in the small squads were killed, the men became increasingly agitated. They met

THE DARK SHADOWS OF VIETNAM

with me and the squad leaders. The guys told us that they didn't want to be killed themselves or to be put in a situation where other guys would be killed, just because the lieutenant would not listen or work with us. "Why is this continuing to happen?" they agonized. "Marines are being killed when it could be prevented!"

Frustrated with the lieutenant and deeply concerned for the safety of my men, I had to deal drastically with the situation. I ignored the chain of command and set up a meeting directly with the next superior officer. But before I could meet with the captain, someone resolved the problem. That evening, outside the camp, the lieutenant was found shot and killed.

An investigation followed, and his death was ruled "killed in action by a sniper." No other truth was ever offered. Subsequently, however, several members of the unit were transferred out.

Fragging happened more often than might be thought. In Vietnam, working with the experienced people, looking out for each other, and listening to other's advice was essential. One's life might depend on it.

On the other hand, in war, a hardheaded, stubborn, arrogant person could just end up fragged.

THE EARS

Some experiences possibly should not be shared. They are too gruesome and graphic for those with weak stomachs. The following story, however, is true and deserves to be told.

During my time in Vietnam, we learned that the North Vietnamese never engaged a unit larger than their own. While our patrols and ambushes were daily and nightly procedures, they were not, unfortunately, always successful.

If a night ambush patrol did not return on time in the morning, we sent out another patrol as quickly as possible to find our fellow marines and friends. On one occasion, with a sense of dread, we were geared up within the hour and out on the trail to find the missing patrol. When we located them, they were all dead and mutilated. To find marines ambushed and killed and left with their testicles in their mouths upset and enraged us.

Angry and frustrated, we radioed back to base for the medical people to come and get the dead men. Wary of the enemy's return, we set up a protective perimeter around the grisly scene. All of us fanned out prone on the ground, spaced about ten feet apart, peering into the surrounding brush and trees. As we listened for any sound that warned of a further attack, we didn't talk. Having daylight, we could see clearly.

When the medics came, they loaded the bodies on stretchers. We helped by picking up the dead men's gear— their rifles, helmets, cartridge packs. Carrying the dead, the medics proceeded back along the trail to the base while our search party covered the rear. No one talked; each man walked alone with his thoughts.

We wanted revenge, payback, and retaliation without mercy. Not knowing which particular NVA group was responsible for the desecration of our marines, when we caught up to any North Vietnamese, we killed them as savagely as possible. Sometimes, with them dead or alive, we cut off their ears. They were going to end up dead in any event. My radioman, a strong kid from Texas, carried a set of ears in a plastic cigarette holder.

About a month after this first incident, our gunnery sergeant asked to see me, as I was the platoon sergeant. He was dealing with a serious situation. He received a letter from our lieutenant, who had received it from a long line of others, starting with police authorities in Texas. They were investigating a mystery, possibly a serious crime.

It seems my radioman, the marine from Texas, had sent his plastic holder of ears home to his mother. When his mother opened the package, the ears fell out. Suffering a heart attack as a consequence, she was rushed to the hospital. Because parts of a human body were involved, the local police were investigating where they came from. The inquiry went right down the line of command and back to my platoon.

Public authorities ranted, expressing horror that such barbaric things should be happening among our troops. How could such abominable behavior be condoned? Military authorities, however, just wanted the problem to go away.

I was enraged with the radioman for sending the ears home. "How could you do such a stupid thing?" I yelled at him. He didn't say much. He had a big heart and a reputation of doing anything for anybody. In this case, he was more concerned about his mother's heart attack.

What happened in our company, then, was that my radioman was transferred from the 3/26th Marines to the Seventh Marines. Later, I heard he was moved several times more. Apparently, no one wanted to get involved or answer questions over the issue of the ears.

Finding bodies mutilated by the NVA happened two or three times in my experience in Vietnam. Certainly, the possession of human ears by a member of the US Armed Forces was bizarre and reprehensible. Nevertheless, the gruesome degradation of fellow marines did explain—if not justify—the wartime escalation of rage.

To this day, I do not know what happened to my ex-radioman, nor do I know what happened to the investigation of the ears.

CHIEU HOI

Chieu Hoi was a risky experiment—an open arms program that ultimately failed. Frequently Viet Cong or North Vietnamese fighters, having seen thousands of their comrades killed and afraid of dying themselves or being sent to a prisoner of war camp, defected from the North to the South. If, after interrogation by the South Vietnamese military, if they had any valuable information, they were assigned to be scouts for the US forces. We relied heavily on their honesty and loyalty, but it turned out they were more interested in staying out of North Vietnam than actually helping us.

I was involved in only one success story using a Chieu Hoi as a scout on patrol. Just outside of Hue, we headed out on a reconnaissance patrol based on information given to us from our Chieu Hoi scout. The fellow had been delivered to our headquarters by the SVN military. As a former Viet Cong, he said he had been to a place that held American prisoners. Our officers sent orders to me and my platoon to investigate. Although we couldn't really trust the Chieu Hoi, it was worth checking out.

Proceeding west towards Laos, we traveled several miles as the area became thick with bushes and trees. We followed the Chieu Hoi down one trail and then off to the right through an area so dense we couldn't see sunlight. That area then opened up to another trail that we followed for about a quarter-of-a-mile to a cluster of outbuildings.

Three structures with bamboo walls and floors stood at right angles to a longer building. In the smaller buildings we found caches of weapons, ammunition, and food like rice and fish heads. The long building, divided into sleeping quarters and a rustic hospital area, contained a small supply of bandages and bottles of first aid treatments. From the hurried disarray in the buildings, it was obvious that the Viet Cong had left within a half a day before.

In front of the buildings, five-by-five-feet square and twelve feet deep, empty pits with bamboo pole covers identified the place definitively as a prisoner of war camp. We couldn't help but wonder if any of our guys had ever been in those pits. The overall conditions were deplorable, crude, and primitive.

To our surprise, when we were ready to leave, the Chieu Hoi told us that there was another place he needed to show us. From his information, we plotted the location on our map. We traveled farther up the same trail. A quarter mile away from the POW location, a stench like no other got so bad we could hardly breathe. A pile of at least two to three hundred dead Viet Cong bodies filled a cave.

From this experience, I saw evidence of what I had heard before about the religion and faith of the Viet Cong and North Vietnamese. They believed that if they die or were killed, not to be buried in their own province was a sin, and their souls were lost. Consequently, soldiers stored the bodies of their dead comrades in caves to come back later and take them home.

After our gruesome find in the cave, we never used any Chieu Hoi again. Although in the south of Vietnam, US forces employed eighteen or twenty units of Chieu Hoi's, it never worked. The Chieu Hoi's could not be trusted. As scouts, they were unreliable, sometimes leading us into ambushes or taking us nowhere. Eventually we shot them as enemies.

After my experience of the cave of dead bodies, I never heard or saw another Chieu Hoi.

CHAPTER 7

A DIFFERENT KIND OF MARINE

During one of our reconnaissance patrols west of Hue, we were scouting areas that we knew the Viet Cong were using as supply routes. We came across a small, remote village of rice farmers that we thought—like other similar villages—might be helping the Vietnamese guerrillas.

To question the people of the villages, a South Vietnamese interpreter accompanied us. He was a quiet guy and an ARVN soldier who did his job for us. The villagers, however, said nothing.

Suddenly, a squad of about fifteen South Korean Marines appeared out of the bush. They were heavily equipped with rifles, pistols, grenades, mortars, and machine guns. Although we recognized them from the patches on their uniforms, their appearance was a total surprise. We did not know they were even in Vietnam. Basically they were like mercenaries: taking orders from neither the US nor South Vietnam but scouting for themselves.

I asked them who they were and what they were doing there. With a slight accent, the sergeant in charge said that they were on patrol. They spoke English and Vietnamese. Seeing us with the villagers, their leader asked me if we needed any help. I told him we had been questioning the villagers with no results. He said, "I'll get you results."

At that time, I did not realize that the Korean Marines had no rules governing their activities. Although they were very polite with us, they were ruthless, cruel, and merciless with the villagers. Four of them took one of the oldest members of the village to question. Shaking the elder and threatening him, they still got nothing out of him. Then they grabbed him, stretched out his two arms, and the leader—with the skill of a surgeon—proceeded to skin the old man.

Crowding around the group of us Koreans and Americans, the villagers—helpless—started screaming and yelling. Barely alive and totally skinned, the old man lay bleeding and dying, as his eyes rolled back in his head. But the torturers were not finished. They grabbed a younger fellow and tied the old man to his back with a rope. Terrified, the young man screamed as the two were dragged down the dirt street in front of the horrified villagers. The rest of the Koreans stood by on alert, ready to control the crowd.

Pulling another old man from among the frightened people, the leader put a knife to the man's throat and told him he was next, unless he started talking. And talk he did. The whole crowd of villagers started babbling at once. Then individually, one by one, they gave us information. They showed us the underground cache of rice and fish and oil as well as weapons like AK-47s and cases of ammunition and grenades stored there by the Viet Cong.

With a self-satisfied smirk on his face but unmoved by the torture of the old man and the panic of the village, the Korean leader asked if there was anything else they could do for us. Replying in the same sarcastic tone of voice I replied, "No, but thanks." They had done what we were not allowed to do.

I was shaken by their barbarity and the fact they had no problem with it whatsoever. To get information, we might have shot the old man, then the next, and the next until we got what we needed. But those Korean Marines were a different kind of marine: ruthless and lawless. They disappeared back into the jungle, continuing toward the west where they had been heading. We had no idea where they were going, and we didn't ask or care.

Before this incident, I had never seen a Korean Marine. After this incident, I never saw a Korean Marine ever again.

THE DARK SHADOWS OF VIETNAM

FALSE AMBUSH

On one unusual patrol at the Khe Sanh, the colonel—who never went anywhere—came along. As far as we field marines were concerned, we never saw our officers; they stayed in the tent headquarters and, were transferred often. But it seemed as if this particular colonel who had never been in the field wanted to see what it was like. With a full pack, he walked through the heavy bush accompanying our complete platoon of marines as we spread out in single file.

We traveled about two miles west of the camp base at the Khe Sanh crossing over a few small hills, before descending into a valley near a large river. Since it was summer, the river—about one hundred feet wide—was nothing but rocks like cobblestones. The locality was heavily wooded, but the river—though lined by dense brush—offered an open area. We hiked to it by way of a small, twenty-foot-wide tributary—itself dry and rocky—stopping about fifty feet from the main river. Suddenly at the mouth of the tributary, two shots broke the quiet.

Anticipating a possible ambush, the lieutenant ordered us to move out of the restriction of the tributary to the river's unobstructed bed where we could see more. I directed three squads to the river mouth—one squad on the left and one to the right—and the third squad remained in the middle to see forward and cover the rear. As we got into position, two more shots alerted us to the possible enemy presence.

Following procedure, I first secured my men before attacking. We had to figure out the possibilities. It might be an ambush. But where, then, was the enemy— to the right, the left, ahead of us? We couldn't respond until we knew what was happening. Nothing happened. I held my position.

Then, as I peered to my right through the small trees and up at a knoll, I could not believe my eyes. The colonel, thinking himself hidden from our sight, stood on the rise, his rifle still in the air after firing it. I knew right then and there he was creating a false impression of an enemy presence. *That dumb SOB!* I thought, immediately recognizing his subterfuge. Squatting low with very little cover, the men of the platoon could see up the river, down the river, and across the river, but—as I well knew—there was nothing to see.

Had I thought that it was a real ambush, I would have sent the guys up and down the river searching for the enemy. But in this case, why would I?

My squad leaders were great marines, each one with a potential for advancement. I directed them to keep their men in their position until we were attacked or until the situation changed. We stayed put for about an hour, but as nothing more happened, the lieutenant ordered us back through the tributary to the Khe Sanh.

Arriving back at the Khe Sanh, we returned to our bunkers in the southwest area of the base. An hour later, the gunnery sergeant—an older guy who had been in the service more than twenty years—told me that I was wanted in the company tent headquarters. He accompanied me there where the lieutenant and colonel confronted me. Unaware that I had picked up on his game, the colonel was annoyed that he didn't get to see any action. Not wanting to embarrass him, I said nothing about having seen him shoot his rifle.

Trying to intimidate me, the colonel demanded an account of my field orders. He wanted to know why I didn't move the platoon, why I kept them where they were. He had thought I would have deployed my men for reconnaissance to scout out the danger.

I told the colonel that, not knowing the situation, protecting my men was my first responsibility. But then, as nothing further had happened, I held my position. By the annoyed tone of his voice, it was obvious the colonel thought I hadn't done enough.

After about a half hour, the colonel dismissed me. When I was leaving, I asked the gunnery sergeant if I could speak with him. Outside I told him the whole story about the colonel staging a false ambush.

"This is Vietnam," I said in no uncertain terms, "and I don't like what the colonel did by playing his

JOSEPH W. BABINE

game. Shooting his rifle could have given away our position to the enemy and really endanger all our lives." I knew I had proceeded in the correct manner by not risking my men when there was no need.

The gunny—a cool guy—had been around the block many times. He knew how to give orders in a way that did not sound like an order but got the men to act right on target. Like myself, he couldn't believe the stupidity shown by the colonel. I know the gunny must have told the colonel what I said and what I knew, because from that time on the colonel treated me very respectfully.

In Vietnam, I was in ten or fifteen real ambushes where we confronted the enemy in various terrains, both of our forces moving like chess pieces to overcome the other. Adjusting tactics at every moment, worrying about the safety of my men, and knowing their lives depended on the quickness and accuracy of my reaction was serious business.

I didn't need to play games like the colonel who created a false ambush.

AIR POWER

Air support played a key role in the northern area of South Vietnam. When I was at the main Khe Sanh base with about six thousand marines, the North Vietnamese forces numbered about seventy thousand. Not only did the RVN attack from North Vietnam, which was eighteen miles away, but also from Laos, only eight miles to the west.

Our base needed air support twenty-four hours a day. The B-52s from Guam and Anderson AFB flew twelve-hour round trips of 5,500 to 6,000 miles. In daytime F-4 Phantoms, F-105 Thunder Chiefs, A-4 Skyhawks, and A-6A intruders covered us.

Night, however, brought the most devastating of the air strikes. When the B-52s came into the surrounding area, they lit up the sky. One day there would be a mountain range, but that night the B-52s would come in and drop their 250 to 1,000 pound bombs. The ground underneath moved and trembled. The next morning, that mountain range was no longer there; instead, there was just a crater. The damage by the B-52s was amazing. The B-52 Strato Fortresses flying between thirty thousand to thirty-five thousand feet high could not be seen from the ground. The pilots used pinpointing radar to hit their targets.

Twenty-five years after I left Vietnam, I was working in excavation. One of the many companies that we worked for was in Contra Costa County. When they were billed, I arranged to pick up their check since I was in the area. For years I dealt with the same manager of that company. We talked to each other all the time. One day I asked what he did before he worked for the company. He told me he was retired from the air force and that during the Vietnam War he was a

B-52 pilot. Amazingly, we had been in Vietnam at the same time.

He told me that being a B-52 pilot had not been easy. The mental strain was extremely hard. He made me aware that as they flew so high they could not be seen from below, and neither did the pilots see their targets. From the beginning, of course, the pilots knew the nature of their missions: to kill the enemy, the North Vietnamese.

I could tell from my friend's voice that when the pilots were flying the Strato Fortresses, they were not thinking about the nature of what the bombs were hitting. He told me after about ten or fourteen missions, many men began to think about the human element of their targets; they might be killing innocent people. This mental anguish forced some pilots to stop flying. They had to receive counseling in Guam and other air force bases. Some men were able to go back to their assignments, but others had to be replaced.

Before my friend and former pilot told me about these reactions, I never even thought about or heard about the mental distress suffered by the men flying those unseen bombers. Although I have always had respect for all our pilots in Vietnam, hearing about the mental suffering they had to go through made me respect them even more.

In Vietnam, all of us—both on the ground and in the air—suffered.

CHAPTER 8

COORDINATES

Since I have always wanted to know where I was, I've found a great appreciation for maps. Maps in Vietnam, however, are unlike maps in the States. In the Khe Sanh, the maps never indicated roads, since there weren't any. They showed no villages and no points of reference, like buildings. A map would indicate dense forest areas, valleys, and rivers and streams.

In Vietnam, coordinates became more important to me. The key to reading a map in Vietnam was in noting the hills and mountains. Reading the mountain ranges, even the ones that were not the specific destination, would tell you where you were. A mapped region consists of straight lines intersecting at right angles to create a network of horizontal and perpendicular lines uniformly spaced that indicate points in the area. The intersection of these lines is the coordinates.

One of our many patrols in the Khe Sanh was planned for the whole company—about forty or fifty men. Besides the machine gun squad, the company included an engineering unit capable of dismantling explosives from booby traps to bombs.

This particular day, the mission was to locate a bomb in a village southwest of our main base at the Khe Sanh. According to our reports, about fifty feet from the village there was a 250-pound bomb that had not exploded. From reconnaissance reports, the village was known as North Vietnamese sympathizers. They supplied the enemy with food and kept a stockpile of weapons and ammunition. They also informed the NVA about US movements.

To get to the village that lay in a valley area, we had to go up and over a few mountains, which were dense with trees and heavy brush. We traveled single file spread out over a mile, but we were still in range to call in our mortars from the Khe Sanh. When the top of the last mountain range opened up, we had a clear view into the valley and the village.

The lieutenant took out his map and said he wanted to call in a 105 mortar barrage from the Khe Sanh to hit the hill next to us. He wanted to use the strike to calibrate the range for the artillery guns. As I pulled out my map and compared it to his reading, I could not believe what I saw— his coordinates were wrong. When I told him so, he looked at me as if I was crazy. "What do you mean?" he demanded. I told him that with the coordinates he was using, his mortar barrage would hit not the neighboring hill but the mountain where we were. To verify my reading, I told him to call in two tracer rounds to the coordinates I gave him, which were for the hill next to us. He did, and we watched the rounds land on the other hill instead of on us. After the tracers landed, the lieutenant handed me his map and said, "Sergeant, you call in the 105 mortars for the village in the valley."

There was no one in the village, even if there had been, they were the enemy, and I could not worry about that. Consequently, the village was destroyed, and we proceeded down the hill into the valley. We searched the village area and found the bomb. After surveying the situation, the engineers determined that the bomb could not be dismantled. It was too far into the ground. The only solution was to set charges and blow it up. We backed off to a safe area. What a dramatic explosion. A cloud of fiery red flames mushroomed straight up from the detonation. The shredded metal of the bomb flew hundreds of meters in every direction. Having seen and felt the effect of many B-52 bombs, we knew enough to stay well back from the burst of power and heat if we wanted to survive.

After completing our mission, the company got ready to return to the Khe Sanh. Then the lieutenant turned to me and said, "Sergeant, take us home." I still couldn't believe the lieutenant had not been able read a map correctly. He should have known where he was. Everyone knew what had happened. From then on, everywhere we went the men would ask me where we were and where were we going. In Vietnam, the wrong coordinates could be deadly.

DEALING WITH DEATH

One time a writer friend read my stories and was impacted by the death and dying I had faced every day in Vietnam— friends being killed, bullets all around me, one guy surviving and another not. He asked, "Do you have a death wish?"

His question made me think. As far as I could remember, never, before, during, or after Vietnam did I have a death wish. Death, however, was all around me.

In war, thinking about death is dangerous. It can keep a person from doing his job, keep him from being aware of what is happening, and keep him from thinking clearly about who and what surrounded him. Psychologically, death had to be shoved to the back of the mind. To do so is not easy, nor can it be done right away. Experience forces one to push away thoughts or fears of death so that situations can be handled. Nobody wants to die, but when death was facing me, I had to deal with it.

Some people could handle recurring death; some couldn't. Reactions to death and danger determined the kind of position to which I could assign a man. Some men would never talk about the death they were witnessing, and others would freak out and back off when facing the threat. Vietnam did not offer any place to escape from confronting death on a daily basis.

In bad or threatening situations, with the panic that rises from the possibility of being killed, individuals in a squad react differently—should they run, take cover, or shoot back? Typically for me, I don't react to difficult situations with anxiety or excitement. Although everything happened fast when a patrol was ambushed, for me, things slowed down.

In the battlefield of Vietnam—keeping my own emotions in hand—I trained myself to take just a matter of seconds to analyze what to do in terms of defense or offense. By giving the men a direct order— even if it was simply "Hit the ground!"—that sense of someone in control neutralized the panic and made them able to respond to the situation in a mindful manner. That I made the right move affected the people around me as well as myself.

In Vietnam, death directly faced me, or I faced death several times. When I was climbing Hill 861, and a bullet hit me in the neck and a grenade shattered my hand, death was a real possibility. Other marines around me were getting shot up and killed—almost all the men in my squad. But I had to keep going. It was no game; there was no chance to call for a time-out.

At other times—as when I stepped on an explosive booby trap on the trail and had to wait motionless in place wondering if it would explode—my life flashed before me. The sensation only lasted a few seconds, but I realized that my life so far had been way too short.

Given so many different death-threatening situations, hardly any two were the same. To say I was never scared would not be the truth. But as to death, I put it out of my mind. Of course, the emotions still operate. To have a fellow marine, a friend, dead in my arms, and to feel the trauma of his death— to see this happening over and over— I had to become hardened. Hardness becomes a habit for survival.

If holding my emotions in check, learning to analyze quickly under attack, and becoming hardened to the dying around me means dealing with death, then I did deal with death. One thing I never had, however, was a wish for death.

THE PURPLE HEART THAT WASN'T

During one trip from Hue to the Khe Sanh, we stopped over in a town south of the base called Quang Tri, in the province of the same name. To avoid psychological fatigue from being in the same place too long, troops were regularly shifted to different fighting areas.

We were relieving the 7th Marines who had been in the area of the Rock Pile for about a month. They had been engaged in flushing out NVA and needed time to regroup and rest.

After about a week in Quang Tri, we planned a big patrol with a full platoon. The platoon itself comprised three full squads with a machine gun section, a lieutenant, and platoon sergeant. Some of the terrain was open with bushy, rolling hills, and our patrol area was not as dense as other sections.

About a mile to a mile-and-a-half out, we were ambushed by a large force of Viet Cong. They were as well equipped as we were—a conventional force in uniform with Russian AK-47s and Chinese machine guns. They also had Chinese advisors who were surprisingly tall and well built. They attacked from the right, almost immediately wiping out our squad on that flank. We were badly outnumbered and called in air strikes.

Before the planes arrived, we had to engage in constant battle using different tactics to hold our position until help arrived. Cover was extremely limited to small hillocks and sparse trees. The air strikes carpeted the enemy with bombs and napalm. With the air attack, many of the VC fled, leaving the rest dead on the upslope.

Significant damage had been done to us. Three-fourths of our platoon was wounded or dead. Our casualties included the lieutenant and the platoon sergeant who were killed along with the many others. I was wounded by a bullet in my left arm.

As the senior sergeant, I had to take over command of what was left of the platoon after the attack. Back in the staging area, I had to get the information from the squad leaders about who had been killed or wounded. By radio, I notified the company commander, giving him the list of the dead and wounded in order to bring in the helicopters to MedEvac the casualties out. From the list of casualties and wounded, the commander would authorize medals and Purple Hearts. I also had to make out a written report on the nature of the ambush—the location and direction of the attack, the enemy numbers, and the need for air strikes.

I made the reports, but I did not include myself on the list of wounded. Even though I could have received a Purple Heart, when I considered all the men who had lost their lives or been seriously wounded, I felt my wound was trivial compared to what they had sacrificed.

From that time on until my tour of duty in Vietnam ended, I remained platoon sergeant, but not with a Purple Heart from that patrol. By personal choice, mine was the Purple Heart that wasn't.

THE DARK SHADOWS OF VIETNAM

CHAPTER 9

HEROES

To me, the word *hero* is used far too often and too loosely.

A hero is a person who is admired not just for achievements, qualities, acts, and ability, but for gallantry above and beyond the call of duty. A hero shows extraordinary ability and skills, but takes it to a new level, putting aside regard for one's own life in order to save others.

Certainly there are heroes, yes, very much so. In critical situations, it is the nature of some people to rely on experience and ability to lead and to take control. In the military, the hero risks his own life to face and defeat the enemy while protecting his own men. But I do not believe any person can *aim* to be a hero. Heroism is an automatic response that happens under a threatening situation. The hero has no fear for his own life. His actions may serve to diffuse a situation, keep it from escalating, or lead him into total involvement with the enemy.

During my military time as a sergeant in charge of many engagements with the enemy, I have been shot at and hit. I know what it is to be scared and frightened. I overcame my fear by putting myself in the right mindset—letting the fear pass to be replaced by a kind of tunnel vision that focuses exclusively on the situation at hand. Nothing else matters.

In order to make the right decisions under pressure, it is essential to be calm and in control. In trouble or in a bad situation, if I keep myself clear-headed, things seem to move in slow motion. This has been true for me both in the military and in life itself.

It seems everyone has a definition of hero. Is being killed heroic? Not all the time. Sometimes a person is in the wrong place at the wrong time. A man becomes a hero, however, when a situation calls him forth to act beyond his personal well-being at the risk of losing his life.

In my mind, to call someone a hero is not done lightly. I believe, for instance, that Audie Murphy is a hero. Among his thirty-three awards and decorations was the Medal of Honor. He received every decoration for valor that this country had to offer—some of them more than once—and he was wounded three times as well.

THE DARK SHADOWS OF VIETNAM

Do I personally know any heroes? Yes, I do: Sergeant Brown of the 3/26th Marines. Brown, a squad leader, was a take-charge man, well-respected and liked. During an ambush at Quang-Tri, his squad was attacked fiercely from the right where the ambush originated. As his Marines hit the ground, he took control of the new situation. He ordered his men to keep firing but to stay put under cover. He himself moved forward, engaging the enemy. Firing his rifle and throwing grenades, he took out about dozen NVA, all the while protecting his men. Unfortunately, Brown ended up being killed. His death hurt me because he had been a close friend of mine for most of that first year in the Khe Sanh.

On the battlefield, I found out a lot about people. I learned about bravery—a quality demonstrated by so many of the men in Vietnam. To be brave is to possess a mental strength that, without confusion, takes care of any situation. A brave man habitually conquers fear and despair in order to stay in control. In harnessing emotions, he is able to respond competently to whatever danger may present itself. In spite of their fear, terror, or confusion on the battlefield, men will respond with readiness to a leader who is brave, who commands with courage and self-control. Furthermore, in so responding, each man also learns about himself. The payoff of bravery is respect.

In Vietnam, I was willing to take charge in difficult situations, and my men appreciated this. I have medals, and my actions have saved some lives. But I do not feel that this makes me a hero. All my life—in the military or otherwise—all I have ever wanted from anyone is respect, not medals or praise. Though I don't need to be liked, I do count on respect.

Yes, there are heroes and brave men, and I have known them.

I THOUGHT I HAD TROUBLE

During my time and years in the marine corps—serving my country and fighting in Vietnam—I was wounded, received medals, and experienced the tough, hard, and bad times of war. I became harder and tougher—more withdrawn into myself—than I had already been. Before I went to Vietnam, I'd already had to learn the hard way about life and growing up. From the age of thirteen years until I went into the marine corps at seventeen, there was no one to talk to me about life or to show me how to deal with it.

When I came back from Vietnam and was discharged from the marine corps, I had a hard time adjusting to normal living. Life was too slow, too quiet. I was used to a life full of the noise of shooting and shouting. I didn't like the system that was trying to tell me what I could and couldn't do: I shouldn't hit somebody in a fight or shoot anyone in anger. For the previous two years, the government had ordered me to fight and taught me to be a killer. Now the same government that had sent me to Vietnam expected me to behave, to live by rules and regulations. Society expected me to conform to its norms and regulations.

Although I got a job and worked hard, my marriage was not working. I had married my wife in California when I was a seagoing marine, but when I was in Vietnam, I rarely heard from her. As for me, I was trying hard just to survive the war; I couldn't afford to give any energy to worrying about her. I think this lack of communication started the downfall of our marriage. I became a drinker. I only drank with the people I worked with, never at home. And I never missed work because of it.

But I didn't know what I wanted or what I wanted to do. Everyone with whom I associated thought I was fine, but inside I was not. I was lonely and had no one to talk to. I was not close to my wife, and to avoid losing someone again, I didn't risk making any friends. I didn't let myself feel sorry for myself. I just threw myself into my work, often for all seven days of the week.

One thing was clear: I did not want anyone close to me. All of my friends—guys close to me in Vietnam— were dead. Brown, Kemp, Williams—to name a few. Their deaths created a void in me. I felt, then, that if I didn't let myself get close to anyone or make any friends, I wouldn't get hurt again or have to suffer another loss. Even today I can count on one hand the number of friends I have—only three: Dennis Lee Thomas, Courtland Layman, and Norman Nesbit. Most of the people I know are merely acquaintances, mainly from my neighborhood. With them I just say hello and act polite.

Although I had had trouble in Vietnam and in other parts of my life, none of it could compare with losing the only one I had let myself get close to after Vietnam. My baby son died when he was almost two. My wife of that time and I tried to fill the emptiness created by the loss of our son by taking in foster children.

Over a two-year period, we took in about six children. They came from families who had drinking and drug problems. No one had helped the children or had shown them how to behave or how to accomplish anything. Their parents were drug addicts and unstable people. With us, however, the children had meals on time, went to school, and were comfortable and grateful for the supportive rules we gave them. But just when they were doing better, the courts would return them to their parents.

Seeing the children who we had loved returned to negligent parents angered us greatly. To us and to the social workers, it seemed that the parents just wanted the children for the welfare money. It was heartbreaking and frustrating to see the children lost in the shuffle. The inadequacy and abuse of the fostering system eventually caused us to withdraw as foster parents.

After Vietnam and the death of my son, I recognized that some problems stay where they were actually experienced, as in Vietnam. Others, though past, endure as painful memories, like that of losing my child. Life goes on, but one doesn't forget.

In my life now, I don't consider anything to be a true problem. When I even begin to think that something is a problem, I remind myself that it's not. I live my life knowing that I can deal with whatever comes along, even though there was a time when I thought I had trouble.

I STOPPED MY WORLD

My son had been born six years after I had returned from Vietnam. At that point, I felt happy and proud. He was my first human attachment since the war. This was the one person I was close to and loved. I felt that he would change me. I liked coming home and playing with him. Because he had Down's syndrome, we had special toys and activities to help his development. For him, everything was a game, and we laughed and played together. But he had medical problems, and less than two years later, he died.

Although it's been thirty-five years since my son died, to this day I am not over his death.

For one whole year, I went to the cemetery every Sunday to visit my son's grave. After months, family members told me that I should not keep going there, but I continued. I could not figure out why they thought they knew how I felt or what I should do. I think they were concerned because I did not talk about the loss but kept my thoughts and feelings to myself as I had always done. Visiting my son made me feel better. The cemetery in Whittier spread out over lovely rolling hills with neat lawns with a chapel capping a rise. I felt comfortable and alive there.

After my son's death, I only took off two weeks, and then I went back to work. But nothing was ever the same—nothing. For the two years following his death, I continued to work and simply exist. I had a good job working for a salary, a house, and a new pickup truck. But there just wasn't anything to look forward to. Every day seemed to be the same.

One spring morning, however, I called up the company I'd been working with for eleven years and told them I would not be coming in. They asked if I was okay and when I planned on coming back to work. I told them that I had decided not to come back, ever. I had been thinking about this for a while, and I had just decided that this April morning was the time. I stopped my world; what I had was over. It was time for me to move on with my life.

Change was something I had to do. I had to think about my life. I wasn't crazy or insane, even though some people thought I was out of my mind. Now was the time to act. I knew where I had been. I also knew where I was, but I didn't know where I was going.

At that time, I was living in Yorba Linda, California. For two weeks I just drove around— no place in mind— from Orange County to Los Angeles. I did not worry about anything. In some way, I knew everything would be all right.

Then I got a phone call from a friend in Northern California— the brother of the guy I had been working for. He had started his own business in Sonoma and asked me if I wanted to come north to work. At that point, I told him no because I had to figure things out in my mind. But a few weeks later, he called back and asked me again. He told me a company in Sacramento needed an excavator and would pay for my airfare and put me up for the weekend. So I said, "Okay, it sure wouldn't hurt anything."

One month later, I had sold my home, moved up north to Vacaville and started working again. Although I had never been to that area of California, it seemed the change was what I needed. I had gotten away from the rat race of Southern California.

The north seemed more open to me, and I enjoyed it. Looking back many years later, I realized that what drove me away from the south was the destruction of open and beautiful places like Yorba Linda. One day I had found myself tearing up a strip of beautiful orange trees for a development. I began asking myself: "What am I doing?"

Even today, I have to step back and look at my life to know where I have been, where I am, and where I am going. It's my way of being me. One thing is clear, when I have to stop my world, I will.

CHAPTER 10

LIFE AFTER VIETNAM

Vietnam was the worst trouble I ever had. Being there hardened me for sure. After six years in the marine corps, I left Vietnam and the corps. I returned home to my wife who I had married when I was a seagoing marine. Following many disappointing miscarriages and many medical consultations, my son, Chad Joseph Babine, was born on September 22, 1972, and I was very happy. He had Down's syndrome, which at that time they called Mongolism. I researched everything I could find on the subject and discovered that it is a genetic disorder associated with the presence of an extra chromosome 21, characterized by mild to severe mental retardation. But I had no problem with accepting his condition.

Chad was mildly afflicted, but they said because of weak muscle tone, he could not walk or sit by himself. He had a hole in his heart that needed to be operated on when he turned two years old. Nevertheless, he was the happiest baby I have ever seen. He smiled and laughed all the time, very rarely crying. He didn't crawl, but he rolled everywhere and fast. Just before he turned two, he caught a cold, and his weak body could not handle the infection. On April 24, 1974, at four in the morning, he passed away. My son's death numbed me. I was in total shock. I couldn't believe that I had lost him, too.

Although two years later we had a healthy son, my marriage dissolved, and I never was able to have much connection with my second boy. Trying to recover financially and emotionally from Chad's death and my divorce, I struggled with bankruptcy and the general recession. It took almost ten years before it started to turn around for me. I worked in an excavation company for a buddy of mine who was the owner. When he retired, he asked me to continue running the company, which I did quite successfully for about fifteen years. Then it was time for me to retire as well.

Today, of my three friends, Corky and Dennis Lee are both Vietnam vets, and Doc is a former corpsman who served in the Gulf War. Although Doc is younger than us Vietnam vets, he is always around with us and talking with us. Corky and I used to play in a band together. Now we enjoy sitting and talking as we listen to music. When I'm with Dennis Lee—who lives next door to me—we talk about life, listen to a lot of music, and help each other. My friends approve of me and help me, as I help them. We support each other no matter what happens.

I think because of what has happened in my life, for me the word *friend* is different than it is for other people. Honesty and feelings are very important. I get along with a lot of people, talk to them, and talk about how they're doing. I like being around people, and I also like being alone. People need to accept me for who I am, as I do other people.

My present wife is a friend I've known for over thirty years. We have feelings of affection, and she is a companion. We enjoy sitting outside and talking or taking trips to Santa Rosa or local festivals or traveling further like Washington state. Most of all, she and I communicate. We talk about everything.

Throughout the years, I have changed, but underneath all my experiences with my family, Vietnam, my business, the most important thing I've learned is to just be myself. I remember all the experiences that have happened to me, and I will not forget them. But my life goes on, and I believe I have become a better person by accepting what comes and not letting myself get riled up by it. I will always say what I think, but then I can walk away. I guess I've learned to have an even keel.

VIETNAM WAR

Many people have written their thoughts and opinions about the Vietnam War. Even though the military engagement in Vietnam was never a *declared war*, I definitely consider it war.

I was a young marine when Vietnam started, and I didn't even know where the country was. But I knew I had to volunteer to go. Now I notice and read about the psychological help available to the veterans of the Gulf, Iraq, and Afghanistan wars. The military has finally recognized the problem of depression brought on by war, as well as the difficulty of dealing with life after returning from war.

But each veteran of Vietnam had to deal with the effects of that war by himself. When we came home, where was help to sort out the mental distress from our experiences? It was left to each veteran to try and find meaning in what he had gone through. Many could not do so, and to this day, still have not done so. Even now, I know veterans who continue to suffer Vietnam-related mental problems.

For myself and many other marines, almost a half century has passed since we left Vietnam. For years I did not talk or write about my experiences. It took me twenty-five years to do so. But writing has helped me understand myself then and myself now.

When we marines, army, navy, and air force personnel went to Vietnam, we went to win a war, and I mean *win*. But after I had been in Vietnam as a sergeant for six months, I and other sergeants realized something was wrong. We were getting orders that did not make sense. We confronted our own lieutenants to find out what was going on—where these ineffective orders were coming from and why. The lieutenants told us that the orders for patrols and ambushes were given to them by the captain who received them from the colonel whom had in turn gotten them from the general at headquarters. We men in the field, then, realized that the generals were not in touch with the actual battlefield realities.

From our field experiences and knowledge of our area, we knew where we should be going in order to find and destroy the enemy. But the higher commanders were issuing us orders to go to places where nothing was going to happen. In that way, there would be limited casualty numbers reported to the American people, which made the higher command appear efficient and effective. For good press back home, fewer body bags meant a better war.

From then on, when we received orders from our lieutenants, we adapted those orders to what we knew could be effective. We mapped out our own patrols and ambushes, even if it meant crossing the border into Laos, which we did many times because it was the main enemy supply line from North Vietnam.

We fighting men were in Vietnam to win a war. But the higher ups in command were being forced to fight a political war in which the priority was to not irritate or upset the upper brass, politicians, government, or president. Many years later, after much personal research, I learned why, who, and for what reason the people in government and the military acted the way they did. Some historians contend that we could have won the war if the politicians had not placed so many limitations on the military effort. I agree with that opinion.

During my time in Vietnam, Lyndon Johnson was President of the United States, and he apparently did not have a clue of what to do about Vietnam. Robert McNamara, Secretary of Defense under John F. Kennedy, continued as Johnson's secretary of defense in 1964. They put Army General William C. Westmoreland in charge of the forces in Vietnam. William Westmoreland and his deputy General Abrams typically bypassed or ignored his staff officers. In my opinion, Westmoreland was a puppet of the politicians and the worst general. As to the commander of the marine corps from 1964-1967, Wallace M. Greene, I—as a marine who was fighting—still don't know or understand where he was or what he did. Meanwhile, all that President Johnson heard from the chief of staff and command was to bomb, bomb, bomb. It seems to me that all these higher ups were in the wrong place at the wrong time.

Although I know one war cannot be compared with another, leadership effectiveness can be compared. In WWII, General Dwight Eisenhower had a great mind for laying out plans and strategy. General Omar Bradley, a great commander in his own right, spent three years with Eisenhower and anticipated what Eisenhower was going to do before it was done. General George Marshall was a take-charge man. General George Patten, a total man of war, did things his own way. A great, forceful leader, he fought side by side with his men. These WWII generals created effective plans, strategies, and tactics to keep the enemy on the defensive at all times.

But Vietnam was a different kind of war; effective tactics and strategies were absent. Around Hue in the south, it was a guerrilla war. In the northeast, Khe Sanh had no offensive objectives. Other than our patrols and ambushes, warfare in the Khe Sanh was a matter of sitting and waiting on the initiative of the RVN. That was no way to win a war.

Before I went to there, I believed in the Vietnam War. During my time in Vietnam, I continued to believe in the war. Even after I returned from Vietnam, I still believed. But when we returned home from Vietnam, there was no welcome for us. People looked at us weirdly; no one cared about us. Over the years, conversations about what happened during the war only take place between veterans because so much of the rest of the nation shut out the war, and us with it.

Originally, I believed the war could be won. It was a war that required an all-out effort, a full commitment to win. But as time passed and people protested, the politicians—wanting to please the people and hold on to their jobs—put limitations on the military. Even the president could not do anything to win the war. So as not to upset the people, he did nothing. Consequently, the war took a turn for the worse. The military dropped the offensive and backed off from attacking the enemy.

By writing this commentary, I am closing my stories of Vietnam. I will never forget, but now, after all this time, I am getting on with my life. Vietnam should never have happened.

GLOSSARY

LOCATIONS

Da Nang: A seaport in central Vietnam off the Gulf of Tonkin formerly known as Tourane.

Ho Chi Minh Trail: A network of jungle paths, winding from North Vietnam through Laos and Cambodia into South Vietnam. Used as a military route by the North Vietnamese to supply the Viet Cong.

Gulf of Tonkin: An arm of the South China Sea west of Hainan. The Gulf is 300 miles long and borders the coast of Vietnam.

Hue: The former Imperial capital of a united Vietnam and current capital of Thua Thien Province, surrounded by the Annamese Mountains, bordered by the DMZ to the north and Laos to the west.

Khe Sanh: The northernmost base of South Vietnam in a remote corner of Quang Tri Province, eighteen miles south of the DMZ abutting North Vietnam and eight miles east of the Laotian border and the Ho Chi Minh Trail.

Quang Tri: South Vietnamese city, capital of Quang Tri Province. To the north is the DMZ and the Democraic Republic of North Vietnam. Quang Tri was a key-point for control of the northern sector of South Vietnam.

Route 9: A dirt or gravel two-lane highway that connects the coastal plain around Quang Tri to the Khe Sanh and Laos.

ORGANIZATION OF TROOP UNITS

Squad: Unit consisting of thirteen marines: three four-man fire teams and a squad leader, led by a sergeant, though most squads were led by corporals or lance corporals.

Platoon: Formed by three squads: In Vietnam a platoon consisted of forty-three marines, but in combat conditions it usually went down to as low as the mid-thirties.

Company: A marine company consisted of 212 to 216 marines. The company included three rifle platoons and a weapons platoon that consisted of nine M-60 machine-gun crews, and three sixty-millimeter mortar crews, plus seven navy hospital corpsmen.

Battalion: About 1,200 to 1,300 marines and sixty naval medical personnel, with four rifle companies, one large headquarters with a supply company plus an artillery battery.

Regiment: Core unit of about 4,000 marines, three infantry battalions, and one artillery battalion.

Division: Large unit of about 13,000 to 14,000 marines including an artillery regiment, three infantry regiments, units of engineers, intelligence, reconnaissance, and supplies.

TERMS AND ABBREVIATIONS

AK-47: Standard issue automatic weapon used by the North Vietnamese Army and the Viet Cong. It fired a 7.62-millimeter bullet at a lower velocity than the M-16 and was much less accurate.

ARVN: Army of the Republic of Vietnam, the military forces of South Vietnam.

Chieu Hoi: Viet Cong or North Vietnamese fighter who defected from North Vietnam to South Vietnam because they did not want to be killed or go to prison. They gave information and were used as scouts. They were very unreliable men.

Claymore Mine: A fan-shaped anti-personnel land mine that used C-4 as its explosive. It produced a fan-shaped pattern of fragments.

Coordinates: A basic system of reference lines for a region consisting of straight lines intersecting at right angles. A network of horizontal and perpendicular lines uniformly spaced pinpointed location points on a map for coordinates.

Corpsmen: Navy medical personnel assigned to marine units. They provided the first medical care received by a wounded marine in the field and on the base. They were highly respected.

DMZ: Demilitarized zone. A zone over three miles wide on both sides of the Seventeenth Parallel that constituted the border between North and South Vietnam.

Elephant Grass: Stalks of bamboo-like grass six to eight feet high, which could cover an entire valley floor. Its sharp edges drew blood.

Fragging: To assault, wound or kill, an unpopular and/or inept officer. The marine corps had forty-three documented fraggings during the Vietnam War.

Gunny: The company gunnery sergeant was usually the highest ranked non-commissioned officer in the field. The gunny had a strong tactical and personnel advisory role.

Hero: A hero is a person who is admired for achievements, qualities, acts and ability, demonstrating bravery above and beyond the call of duty in order

118

to save others, with no regard for his own life, thus taking gallantry to its highest level.

Helicopters

Chinook: CH-47 helicopter, heavily used in the Vietnam War. Capable of carrying twelve tons of supplies and troops.

Seaknight: CH-46 twin-rotor helicopter, used by the marines for assaults, resupply, and MedEvacs. It had a ramp at its tail where marines got on and off.

I Corps: "Eye Corps." First geographically listed allied tactical zone encompassing five northern provinces of South Vietnam.

M-16: Standard issue automatic rifle used by the US Army and Marines during the Vietnam war. It fired a 5.56-millimeter bullet at a very high velocity. It is still in use.

MedEvac: A process for evacuating the wounded from a battle field by helicopter.

Napalm: A highly incendiary jelly-like substance used in firebombs, very hot.

NVA: North Vietnamese Army, a well-equipped and well-trained regular fighting force.

NV: North Vietnam

Planes

> F-4 Phantoms
> F-105 Thunder Chiefs
> A-4 Sky Hawks
> A-6A Intruder
> B-52 Strato-fortress

Point: The first man, the scout, in front of a column, "The Point Man" or just "The Point."

Reconnaissance: Small unit of men used to search for useful military information in the field, usually in enemy territory.

Semper Fi: Short for Semper Fidelis, Latin for Always Faithful, the marine corps motto. For marines it primarily means always faithful to each other.

SV: South Vietnam

VC: Viet Cong: The guerrilla army based in South Vietnam, supplied by the North Vietnamese and fighting against the ARVN and the U.S. forces.